When Love is Not Enough

A Guide to Parenting Children

with

Reactive Attachment Disorder-RAD

by Nancy L. Thomas,
Therapeutic Parenting Specialist

Library of Congress Card Number: 00-191847
ISBN: 0-9703525-0-6

This book is lovingly dedicated to my husband, Jerry ,
who has stood at my side and shared his hugs
through every battle for each child's life.

Acknowledgements

I want to thank all the people who have taught me throughout the years, and helped me with the children as I put this program together: Foster Cline MD, C.J. Cooil MSW, and Therapeutic Mom, Lori Wilson, The hours we have spent helping these children together is in the thousands. Many of these techniques were developed by these loving people, who were kind enough to teach them to me in order to help the children and their families.

I owe a great debt to my husband and my children, who gave so much of themselves for years to help me in my endeavors to offer opportunities for the wounded children to heal: Robert, (RB) my strong son and his loving wife Kymm, Clifford, from whom I learned so much, Terena, who was my loving and incredibly competent right arm for many years, Beth, who lights up my life with her love, and now, Adam, very new on the scene, but guaranteed to keep it from getting boring.

I want to thank all those who encouraged and supported my work on this book by their friendship, editing, and typing skills: Helen Bandarra, Mari Damsma, Jack Jabbour, Jim Leuthauser and Cheri Murray.

Last but not least I thank all of the families wounded by Attachment Disorder, ADD, ADHD, Bipolar Disorder and Tourette Syndrome that I have been blessed to meet and work with over the years. You all remain in my prayers and in my heart. I have learned from every child and every parent I have worked with. I thank you all from my heart.

The dog looked at the man and said
"you feed me, you love me, you pet me,
you clean up after me, <u>you</u> must be God."

The cat looked at the man and said
"you feed me, you love me, you pet me,
you clean up after me, I must be God."

author unknown

This book is for those of you who have kittens.....
with claws.

Table of Contents

PART I: THE PROBLEM

America's most valuable resource is its children; today we are tossing them aside at an unprecedented rate. (McKelvey, C. & Stevens, J. Ph.D. 1994)

For simplification the term "he" will be used throughout this text to refer to the child whether male or female. The broken heart of Attachment Disorder does not have a preference for either gender. ADD, ADHD and Tourettes is more common in males.

Please, Read this Intro. First!!

Let the child's first lesson be obedience, and the second will be what thou wilt.
— Benjamin Franklin

The tools and techniques presented in these pages took two decades to collect and hone into a highly successful healing program for children with problems, such as Attachment Disorder, ADD, ADHD, Tourette's Syndrome and bipolar. These conditions require specialized parenting techniques to give the child an opportunity to develop into an honest, decent, loving adult. These techniques have been proven to be highly successful with tough kids, even kids who have killed, if completed lovingly. Normal parenting techniques such as lecturing, grounding, star charts, removing privileges that may work with normal children are not successful with children who have severe behavior problems. This book was written for ABUSED PARENTS!

I do not have a PhD in psychology. What I do have is a mom's heart and a mom's hands. I started with the same thing you are starting with, a desire to help children. I have parents who call me from all over the US and Canada that are broken-hearted, wounded, and bleeding as they share their story of a lost dream of loving a child to health. Love is *not* enough. This guide is my gift to you. In this book I share the methods and actions I have used for over twenty years to heal disturbed children, some even psychopathic. My definition of success is a child who is respectful, responsible, and fun to be around at school, in the community and most importantly at home. I don't have a special gift. I don't have anything that you, holding this book don't have. With the following tools, your continued love, and the expertise of an attachment therapist, you can heal the broken hearts of children and make them whole.

The tools in this book are most effective with children from toddlers to the onset of puberty (approximately twelve years old). Once puberty hits, the child's focus becomes one of becoming independent, firming up their own belief systems. It is a time of separating rather than a time of connecting. This book is about the human connection. The success rate is low for teenagers unless the teen is asking for help. Healing a teen is NOT a hopeless situation once puberty has begun. There is always hope and an opportunity to save a child as long as they are breathing!

In a two-parent family, the child bonds with both the mother and the father. The bond with the father is a very important part of their life and their learning. The father's job from the infant's view is to protect the family and to teach the child how to handle the outside world. The mother's job from an infant's perspective is to keep the child safe and to teach them about the heart-to-heart relationship between people. The bond between the mother and the child is the one I am addressing when dealing with attachment problems. The connection with the mother is the bond that becomes traumatized and must be healed. There are fathers who do the maternal bonding with the children and are actually the "moms" due to the absence of one parent. When using the term "mom," I don't mean male or female, I mean the primary adult caretaker in the child's life. It does not have to be a female. That offends some people, but from the child's view point, that's the way it is.

Who is the real mom? Is it the one who gave them birth? Not necessarily! Some of these children have had ten or more moms! The real mom is the one that guides their way, picks them up when they fall down, holds them when they cry, and loves them no matter how bad their behavior becomes. Sometimes, this may be the foster mother, the adoptive mother, the step mother or the grandmother. If the birth mother is called the real mom, is the current mom then fake? It must be clear to the child who the real mother is! She then will become the target of their anger and the haven for their hearts to heal.

I have found, with the children that I have lived with, and helped to heal, if the father has stabbed, raped, beaten, or even in one case run over his own child with a truck, the children blame the mom for not protecting them. If the mother divorces the father for being abusive, drinking, or not supporting the family, the children are angry with the mom, not the father. She becomes their target for revenge. A puppy, lying in the road injured, upon being moved, often bites the person trying to get them medical assitance. This is because moving the injured pup causes them pain due to the earlier trauma. Just as the puppy mistakes the helper for the abuser, so does the injured child. A child who has been hurt, by being separated from or abused by one mom, will seek vengeance on the next mom. Thus, the mom is the one the child hates and therefore abuses. These children are clever, sneaky and manipulative. The father and other people often do not even see the abuse the child inflicts upon the mother.

With this book I offer you the skills to defend yourself, to bring laughter and peace back into your home, and to renew your dreams of having a loving child. I worked with a nine year old boy who had stabbed his two year old sister to death, with no remorse. He is now seventeen years old, functioning well in a normal family and graduating from high school. He's not on drugs or in prison which was his original destination, due to the abuse he suffered as a toddler. He took the opportunities to heal that were offered to him and used them to change his cold heart into a caring one, as many of the other children I have worked with have done. You can have a child who knows how to have a loving relationship, rather than a lifetime of loneliness. It is still possible to have a child who has notable work skills and can be successful as an adult in the job market. Rather than repeat the cycle of abuse, you can have a child who will hold, love, and teach his own infants . One day your child could look into your loving eyes and say, "Thank you, for all you've done for me. I love you!" and mean it with all his heart. The task of healing the heart of a broken child is not an easy one. It takes months of thankless, heart rending labor to deliver a disturbed child into the world with a loving heart. There is nothing that can compare with being part of the moment when your child reaches for love and lets it shine into their heart and soul.

Stay Cool ! Fight Fire With Water.
Put out the fire of their rage with your waves of love!

CHAPTER ONE: UNDERSTANDING THE PROBLEM

A child is a curly, dimpled lunatic.
— Ralph Waldo Emerson

What is Attachment?

Attachment is defined as the affectional tie between two people. In this guide book it refers to the bond between the infant and mother. This bond becomes internally representative of how the child will form relationships with the world. Bowlby stated "the initial relationship between self and others serves as blueprints for all future relationships." (Bowlby, 1973)

What is Attachment Disorder?

Attachment Disorder is defined as the condition in which individuals have difficulty forming lasting relationships. They often show nearly a complete lack of ability to be genuinely affectionate with others. They typically fail to develop a conscience and do not learn to trust. They do not allow people to be in control of them due to this trust issue. This damage is from being abused or physically or emotionally separated from one primary caretaker during the first 3 years of life. "If a child is not attached-does not form a loving bond with the mother-he does not develop an attachment to the rest of mankind. The unattached child literally does not have a stake in humanity."(Magid & McKelvey 1988) They do not think and feel like a normal person. " At the core of the unattached is a deep-seated rage, far beyond normal anger. This rage is suppressed in their psyche. Now we all have some degree of rage, but the rage of psychopaths is that born of unfulfilled needs as infants. Incomprehensible pain is forever locked in their souls, because of the abandonment they felt as infants." (Magid & McKelvey 1988) "There is an inability to love or feel guilty. There is no conscience. Their inability to enter into any relationship makes treatment or even education impossible."(Bowlby 1953) Some famous people with Attachment Disorder that did not get help in time: Adolph Hitler, Saddam Hussein, Edgar Allen Poe, Jeffery Dahmer, and Ted Bundy. One famous person with Attachment Disorder who did get help in time (in 1887!), and became one of the greatest humanitarians, is Helen Keller.

What is *Reactive* Attachment Disorder?

In 1980 the Diagnostic and Statistical Manual of the American Psychiatric Association (DSM III) added the term "reactive" to what Foster Cline MD had termed "Attachment Disorder" in 1979. At that time the DSM III manual used " Reactive Attachment Disorder " (RAD)to include only those children suffering from Attachment Disorder under the age of eight months. It was updated in the DSM III revision to include older children. It is now called Reactive Attachment Disorder of Infancy or Early Childhood (313.89). Thus at this point the terms are used inter-changeably. I prefer the shorter version Attachment Disorder or the acronym RAD.

What Causes Attachment Disorder?

Bonding begins at conception. The "in utero" experience has a direct effect on the bonding ability and personality of the child. Drug or alcohol exposure, maternal stress or an unwanted pregnancy can damage the developing child. Babies *do know* what the mother is thinking and feeling during pregnancy. (Verny 1981)

Any of the following conditions occuring to a child under 36 months of age puts a child at high risk for Reactive Attachment Disorder:

physical, emotional, or sexual abuse

neglect

sudden separation from primary caretaker (ie illness or death of mother or severe illness or hospitilization of the child)

inadequate day care; or change of day care provider

undiagnosed or painful illness, such as ear infections or colic

chronic maternal depression

several moves and /or placements (foster care, failed adoptions)

unprepared mothers with poor parenting skills

These situations can cause the child to "shut down" and not develop the ability to trust, love, or care. The child then allows no one to control them. They must be in control, manipulate, and they have little or no conscience development.

The First Year of Life

The focus of the first year should be on the infant's needs and meeting those needs. It is a time of _enthroning_ the infant, as their needs become a priority for the parents. The human infant is the most helpless and hopeless of any living thing born. When they have a need, such as food, warmth, touch or pain relief, they cry for help. The cry they use quickly turns into a rage as the child, in his helpless, hopeless state, has an honest fear of dying if needs are not met. By the time the child is seven days old the attachment between the primary caretaker (mother) should be such that the baby's cries and non-verbal communication are clearly understood. (Verny, 1981) When the caretakers are switched, such as in the case of foster care, day care or hospitalization, the new caretakers do not know the child's language. When the infant cries for warmth, the new caretaker, unable to decipher the child's cries for help, will often meet the wrong need. The baby's cries for help when met correctly with eye contact, touch, smiles, movement, and basic carbohydrates, leads to trust and bonding. This basic trust is the beginning of the development of a conscience. (Cline 1982) Conscience is what helps us choose right over wrong, what helps us to care about others' feelings, and stops us from hurting or killing each other.

High Risk Signs in Infants

Weak crying response or constant crying
Tactile defensiveness (flinching or startling after 8 weeks of age)
Poor clinging or holding on
Resistance to cuddling: seems "stiff as a board"
Poor sucking response
Poor eye contact, lack of tracking (following)
Developmental delays
No reciprocal smile response (they don't return the smile)
Indifference to others (no "stranger anxiety" after 6 months of age)
Self abuse (head banging, etc.)

Keys to Bonding for High Risk Infants

For babies that have had one or more of the high risk factors listed on page seven, the plan for rebuilding the broken bond for infants includes the following:

Breast feed if possible
Always hold bottle (NEVER prop it)
Carry the baby in a snugli on the front, facing mom four to six hours daily
Massage baby 20 minutes each day while smiling and using high voice
Hold and rock infant with loving eye contact, smiles and singing or reading in happy "baby talk" each day
Feed sweet milk in Mom's arms with soft eye contact, touch (stroke baby's face, hold fingers) loving voice.
Baby should nap daily, resting skin to skin on Dad's chest
Baby should sleep with or near parents at night. Be careful to avoid falls.
Do not allow baby to self feed
No "baby carrier," baby is carried in loving arms
No stroller facing away from Mom
No one feeds the baby except Mom
No one holds baby except for Mom and Dad unless less than five min/day
Baby must not be left to cry alone for longer than three minutes
Hold baby facing you-heart to heart
No exposure to TV for one full year
Delay painful medical procedures, if possible, until child is fully bonded
Play Mozart's music to soothe baby
Respond to baby's attempts to get your love and attention with joy!!!

Every minute you invest holding your child and smiling into their eyes is ONE HOUR less pain when they are teens. If Mom must be away four or more hours a day, she must hire someone for the baby to bond to. This person becomes primary and must remain in the baby's life for the first three years to prevent a bonding break during this crucial time.

I recommend the following excellent informative video with fascinating footage on infants:

To order <u>The First Years Last Forever</u>
Send your name, address and $5 to
I Am Your Child
1010 Wisconsin Ave, NW, Suite 800
Washington DC 20007
or phone 202-338-4385

Here's another outstanding video resource that explores ground breaking research from the last three decades and how it can dramatically influence infant care.

<u>Amazing Talents of the Newborn</u>
Available through the Johnson & Johnson Pediatric Institute
877-565-5465 Fax 877-565-3299

The Second Year of Life

The focus of the second year of life, between first and second birthday, should be on limit setting by the primary care giver. It's the year of _de_throning. The concept of "NO" and accepting limits must be developed. The child wants to have and do things, such as play with the knobs on the stereo. An effective parent sets the limit by saying "no" and meaning it. The bonded child with adequate conscience development sees the displeasure in the parent's eyes, stops playing with the knobs of the stereo, and then sees pleasure in the parent's eyes. This is how children learn to accept limits. "This cycle of want - limit setting - accepting limits repeats many times a day during this second year. The toddler earns more freedom and autonomy by accepting limits."(Cline 1982) This teaches the child to control themselves and obey the rules of society. "Effective discipline of toddlers lays the moral foundation for most future behavior." (Cline 1982)

When the first year cycle has broken down it is extremely difficult, if not impossible, to set limits and have the child accept them because they do not trust. These children are stuck in the "I want" mode. They consistently break the rules. Sometimes, for whatever reason, the cycle of setting and accepting limits is not taught by a loving parent. The parents try to change the world to fit the child rather than train the child to fit into the world.

Toddlers with ADD, ADHD or Tourette Syndrome often wear the parents to exhaustion by testing the limits. These exhausted parents give up control and lose the battle, feeling it's easier to ignore behavior than to correct it. Keeping limits set and the boundaries strong during this time is difficult but has great rewards to reap for the rest of the child's life. Toddlers allowed to be out of control because the parents have no control will not bond to an adult they see as weak. A toddler that can manipulate or outlast an adult in their testing phase soon learns not to trust.

Along with the following basic training, we highly recommend, parents of toddlers that are at high risk for Attachment Disorder follow the guidelines outlined in Holding Time by Martha Welsh, MD. , published by Simon & Schuster, 1988

Basic training that should be learned by 18 months of age

come, when called the first time
go, to room or wherever sent
no means NO-not continue to test limits or start whining and arguing
sit
stay where you are told (in your chair, car seat, play area, etc.)

CHAPTER TWO: ATTACHMENT DISORDER - THE PARENT'S PERSPECTIVE

Do what you can -with what you have -where you are.
-Theodore Roosevelt

Parents feel great pain having a child that rejects their love. They often feel like bad parents. "When parents of unattached children--often children who have suffered early abuse and neglect--are taught child management techniques and then conscientiously carry them out only to see them fail again and again, a sense of futility sets in. Parents then feel increasingly more hopeless.(Cline1982)

The feelings of guilt and shame the parents are burdened with, as the child injures other children and pets, defies authority, and is destructive to things around them, are very painful and destructive themselves. The community looks for someone to blame rather than a solution to the problem. Finding someone to blame does not help! It is vital to let go of the guilt, let go of the shame and resolve to solve the problem. Whether another parent is the one that broke your child's heart or you made the errors yourself is of no consequence anymore. Laying blame will not help heal the child. Carrying guilt and shame wastes a tremendous amount of energy that could be put to much better use healing the child. Yes, the child can heal.

The loss of the dream of having a child to hold and laugh with and teach wonderful things can be heart rending. Parents set their sights and their goals toward having a normal, healthy, loving relationship filled with laughter and fun, and then disillusionment, pain and heartbreak drown the dream. It is hard to keep a dream alive as you daily watch the child destroying it. You don't have to give up your dreams! There will be a "slight delay" as you adjust the heart-to-heart connection with your child and get them back on track. The "slight delay" is in terms of your child's life span. The delay will last between six months and two years, depending on how old your child is and how disturbed. It is well worth the effort to get your dream back on track and to have a child to hold and teach and laugh with. In my experience once a child, who has been without love because they have rejected it for years, embraces it again, he has a greater capacity for love than a child who has never been without it. It is like the rainbow after the storm. The storm of an Attachment Disordered child can drown your dreams or you can use this guide book as your boat and take up water skiing!

A PARENT'S VIEW: THREAT OR WARNING SIGN?

You can view your child's unacceptable behavior in one of two ways; a "Threat" or a "Warning Sign". A skunk lifts its tail in your direction to warn that you are too close. Incorrect action on your part may result in being sprayed. Incorrect response to a child giving warning signs will also cause a big stink and make your eyes run.

If you consider the bad behavior a threat, you are in danger as well as your home. Threats and attacks come from enemies. If you come to think of your child as an enemy, that is what they may very well become. With attacks on yourself, your home, and your possesions, will come anger. These children feed on anger. They want you as rageful on the outside as they feel on the inside. When you get angry they "chalk one up" on their score card. Anger makes them sicker and does not do you any good either! Give it up. Decide to no longer let your child "make you angry"!

If you look upon your child's unacceptable behavior as a warning sign (such as danger ahead or sharp curve), then you should take necessary action. If you see your child's destructive/defiant actions as warning flags, you can stay more objective and maintain a sense of perspective. I like to actually visualize them waving a flag crying, "Help me! Help me!" when I find items broken or stolen. Then, rather than getting angry, I get busy working on the bonding. Action not anger! Being warned, you can take action and make a positive impact on your child's life.

The way you perceive your child's behavior will influence the way you act and react. Your choice, threat or warning, will have a direct influence on how your child sees himself. You can view him as the evil aggressor or as one who needs your help.

To succeed you must consider your child's behavior as a warning flag that requires you to take action. You must believe there is, deep inside, a loving child, good and kind, in need of your help. With these specialized parenting techniques it is possible to turn a child, who has even already killed, into a loving, giving child with appropriate development of conscience.

The cause of your child's unacceptable behavior may include one or more of the following conditions:

1. Reactive Attachment Disorder (RAD)
2. Attention Deficit Disorder (ADD)
3. Attention Deficit Hyperactivity Disorder (ADHD)
4. Tourette Syndrome (TS)
5. Adoption problems
6. Overindulgence (Parents trying too hard to make the child happy)
7. Bi-polar Disorder

The above conditions often inhibit or eliminate the healthy relationship between parent and child. The foundation of the child's mental health is that heart-to-heart connection. In dealing with the symptoms, one must also deal with the cause. A broken bond creates an inability to trust, so that responsible adults are forbidden to be in charge. The specialized parenting techniques in Part II have been very effective with each or a combination of these conditions. In many of these conditions proper medications are required in order for the child to be able to function. This book is not a replacement for therapy or a doctors care. Have a skilled professional on your team. In ALL of these conditions special parenting skills are necessary.

Protect Your Pets!

CHAPTER THREE: ATTACHMENT DISORDER - THE CHILD'S PERSPECTIVE

In order to understand what an unattached child feels, one must understand his perspective. Imagine that you are the young child who must cross a frozen lake in the autumn to reach your home. As you are walking across the lake alone, you fall suddenly and unexpectedly through the ice. Shocked and cold in the dark, you can't even cry for help. You struggle for your very life. Alone, helpless, and hopeless without the very air you need to breathe for life, you struggle to the surface. Locating the jagged opening, you drag yourself through to the air and crawl back into the woods from where you started. You decide to live there and never, never to return onto the ice. As weeks go by you see others skating and crossing the ice, you become clearer in your perception that the ice hates you alone, and if you go out onto it, you will die.

Your family across the pond hears the sad news that the temperature will drop to sub-zero this night. So a brave and caring family member searches and finds you to bring you home to love and warmth. The family member attempts to help you cross the ice by supporting and encouraging, pulling and prodding. You, believing you will die, fight for your life by kicking, screaming, punching and yelling (even obscenities) to get the other person away from you. Every effort is spent in attempting to disengage from this family member. The family member fights for your life, knowing you must have the love and warmth of home for your very survival. They take the blows you dish out and continue to pull you across the ice to home, knowing it's your only chance.

The ice represents the strength of the bond and your ability to trust. It was damaged by the break in your connection to someone you trusted. Some children have numerous bonding breaks throughout their young lives. This is like crashing them into the ice water each time they are moved, scarring and chilling their hearts against ever loving and bonding again.

The following was written by Beth, a 15-year-old healed RAD and ADD child, to help you understand :

> When I had my first adopted mom I was scared of her. I was scared of what she would think of me if I wasn't her perfect child. I was so scared, that I just figured instead of being the perfect child and trying to put on a flawless show, why should I? I might as well not try because I'm going to screw up anyway. Deep down I wanted

her to love me, but I also didn't. Because if she loved me I wouldn't be able to take it. My birth mom loved me and then died so why should I let this woman love me when I know that if she does, she will probably just disappear or die also. No way was I going to let someone get close to me again. I pushed and pushed until she had no idea what was going on.

To every other person I was a charming, adorable little child with big blue eyes. How could this child be disturbed? She's just a little girl! Yeah, just a little girl with a solid rock for a heart. Just a little girl with rage smoking from my ears. But, no; that can't be! She's so sweet when she's with us. She is just fine. Oh yeah, I'm just fine because you are too blind to see what I can do to you. Yeah, I'm so shy and so angelic, what could ever be wrong at home. That's because you don't know how powerful I am! Look what I've done to you. I've made you feel sorry for me and want to shower me with affection. Oh, I'm so smart. Now don't you start to love me or you too will get the power of my wrath. You too will know what I hide so well from the outside world. If you love me, I will die. No, no, No!

Baby sitters were no match for me. I was a five year old, thirty pound terror. They would do anything to get me to shut up or calm down. Anything! I would lie and say my mommy and daddy hated me, that they didn't care. Then when sent to go to bed, I would howl and holler for my "mommy". Of course I didn't care whether my "mommy" lived or died. Actually I did care, I cared if she lived, I didn't want her to live. If she lived, I would die.

I had to be powerful, I had to be the one in charge. To be in charge, I had to hide my fear of love, so I covered it with hate. I hated that mom so much that she, herself, was scared of me. So scared that she looked for help, she couldn't take it anymore, and I had won. Yes! I am strong, I am powerful, and no one, not anybody can ever break the steel covering I have over my heart. No one can ever touch me again. I have succeeded.

When I turned six, I was even worse. I had pushed my mom and my dad away. My little brother was terrified of me. I was a demonic queen! I knew for sure I was a witch. I knew I had to have power to control all these people, to push everyone away and make no one like me. I was never lonely, and if I started to be, I'd quickly do something mean to make myself feel strong.

Then they found help. But I believed it wasn't going to work. I could be the sweetest, most agreeable and pleasant child. No one could stop me. Whoa, was I in for a shock! These people knew! These people could see right through me. Aaah! This wasn't right. I can't work with these people; they know too much. Quick, I had to get out of here. No, don't you hold me! Let me go !! NO! NO! NO! You will never know what I am like deep down inside. I am a witch, a powerful demon. You can't stop me.

Oh, it was painful. They were breaking down my walls of steel. They knew how scared and sad I was. No one else did. They knew how mad I was at my birth mom for dying. No one else did. They knew I blamed my little brother for killing my birth mom. No one else did. They held me and made me scream and tell things that I did not want to tell, but I did. They pried into my soul and made me talk about the sad and scared and mad. I didn't want to, but I did. They helped me be strong in a good way. I was powerful, because I was in charge of no one but me. That made me powerful because I had power over myself. Before, my emotions and mind just took over my body. I was actually turning into a happy child. I was learning that I could trust somebody, that they weren't going to die on me, and if they did, I was going to be okay.

I was becoming a loving child. I actually could feel love. It was so scary at first. I didn't want it. But, it felt so good. It was so soft and gentle and kind. I had never felt this before, and now that I had, I could relax for once and let someone else take care of me. I could just be a little girl who loved myself and loved my mom and dad and little brother. I could just let it go. I didn't have to be a witch with strong powers. I didn't have to hate people and push them away. I could just be.

So, that's what I did, and here I am writing this for you to read at the age of fifteen in a family who loves me dearly. I live in a new family because I had pushed my other family away too long and too hard, so they decided to relinquish rights. I live in the family who helped me to live, who helped me to love. Please, I beg of you to understand how I felt and how *your* child feels. Please stay with them and love them along the way. The road will be long and rocky with so many pot holes. Don't worry. It will become smooth once again. They will one day look into your eyes and tell you "Thank you. I love you!" Like I did.

Here's a picture of me with my dog, Stryder at Easter. I made it and your child can too!

CHAPTER FOUR: SIGNS AND SYMPTOMS OF ATTACHMENT DISORDER

For a complete check list of Signs and Symptoms of RAD (Reactive Attachment Disorder) see Appendix B . Even normal children will have periods during which they will have a few of these symptoms. The diagnosis calls for more than half of the symptoms.

The annotated list of signs and symptoms of children who have RAD are they:

1.   Act superficial and phony, especially around strangers or people they feel they can manipulate in order to be in control. (They call them suckers)

2.   Avoid eye contact with people who love them unless they are lying, or conning, then they make excellent eye contact.

3.   Indiscriminately affectionate with strangers. They do not go through the healthy stranger anxiety period an infant goes through. As older children they hug strangers and school principals and anyone else they feel they can get on their side, against their mom.

4.   Lack ability to feel real, from their heart, caring. Giving and receiving affection is not possible without trust. They are called the trust bandits (Magid/ McKelvey, 87). These kids are not cuddly or snugly. (stiff hugs)

5.   Extreme control problems worsen as the child gets older. They want to do things their way right or wrong! They are very sneaky.

6.   They leave a trail of destruction with other kids, pets and even their own body. Albert Schweitzer once said, "Anyone who has accustomed himself to regard the life of any living creature as worthless is in danger of arriving also at the idea of worthless human lives." "The criminal 'Hall of Shame' is filled with people who as children did nasty things to pets. If their parents or teachers had seen the warning signs or known how to counsel them, history might have been different. Animal abuse is not just a warning sign of a future adult criminal- it's a signal a child is deeply disturbed and

needs help" (Mike Capuzzo Rocky Mountain News, 3/5/94) Some of the children I have worked with have raped, injured or even killed numerous animals before someone even suspects it might be the child! Dr. Cline calls pets in the home of the unattached "endangered species."

7.   Lying is a dedicated hobby for RAD children. They often become masters at crazy, twisted stories, outright fabrications, and distortions of the truth.

8.   Impulsiveness is common. They see something and they want it. They steal it, or they do it. There is little or no forethought.

9.   Learning lags and disorders are created by the agitated emotional state they are constantly in as well as an inability to do it the teacher's way (that requires trusting that the teacher's way is the right way). They actually believe if they do it someone else's way, someone else wins and they lose. No one wants to lose! They think they are winning when they do it their own way. Everyone loses when that happens.

10   Cause and effect thinking is learned during the first year. They cry, mom comes, things get fixed(hunger/cold etc). The broken cycle creates the problem of not putting together- I run in the road, a car comes, I die. They don't get it.

11. A conscience is the little voice in your head saying, "No! don't do it, you'll feel bad, or someone else will feel bad". These kids often have not developed a conscience. They can kick the dog, and it makes them feel powerful. Strangling a cat, because they have no empathy for living things, is just something to do.

12. They often have abnormal eating patterns: starving themselves or gorging.

13. Other children do not want to be friends with them because of their need to control, their lack of conscience, and their cruelty to others. They become loners and, without treatment, live a very lonely life of broken or nonexistent relationships.

14. The infantile rage they often internalize that first year, instead of internalizing a loving parent, makes them fascinated with destruction, fire, blood, gore and evil. They often identify with the devil.

15. Normal people talk for two reasons: to communicate thoughts or feelings. Attachment Disorder kids talk for three reasons: to interrupt, make noise, or control. They do not use language to connect. They use it to manipulate and play games, aka (jabbering). Nonsense questions pop out lots.

16. They can be inappropriately demanding and clingy, usually to be "cute" for strangers, or to get something they want.

17. Normally, verbal communication starts with hearing the patterns of our birth mother's voice, which we seek when we are born. Attachment Disorder children have abnormal speech patterns. They have you saying "what?" all the time, because they refuse to speak clearly. When you speak they say "What?" Many of them are in speech therapy for years with a caring teacher. They are not interested in learning communication skills.

18. These kids love to tell lies about alleged abuse to authorities by the people who love them. It makes them feel powerful when they are believed. They *are* powerful! This is one of those cases where you are guilty until you prove your innocence. How do you prove you *did not do* something?

19. Having adults united on one team is very threatening to children who do not trust. In order to be in control they divide and conquer by pitting one adult against the other. Sometimes it's even father against mother or teacher against parents, therapist against parents, etc.This is called "Triangulation".

20. Parents of Attachment Disorder children often appear unreasonably angry. Probably because the more they love their child, the more pain the child dishes out to get them to stop. The child believes love hurts, as it did when his heart were broken as an infant. They don't use the parents' love to grow emotionally strong. Parents are basically abused in their own home.

CHAPTER FIVE: THERAPY FOR ATTACHMENT DISORDER

Luck equals preparation meeting opportunity
-Raymond Wayne Hightower

Attachment therapy and holding therapy are the only therapies that have proven to be effective with Attachment Disordered children. Holding Therapy, as defined in <u>Don't Touch My Heart</u> by Mansfield and Waldmann, is "a psychotherapeutic technique during which the child is cradled to ensure safety and to provide nurturing". "The failure in treatment of all those who had suffered rejection or who never had a loving relationship recalls Dr. Goldfarb's remark that he has never seen "even one example of a significantly favorable response to treatment by traditional methods of child psychiatry." (Bowlby 1953) Ineffective therapy, such as talk therapy or play therapy, relies on establishing a relationship with the client, gaining their trust and processing the problem. *These children do not have the ability to establish a relationship or to trust.* The correct treatment must use the mother as the change agent. Since the bond is damaged between the parent and child, it must be repaired there. The mother must be empowered with the right techniques in order to control the child. The child will not learn to trust someone weaker than themselves. If they can control and manipulate the adult, they are stronger. The adult MUST be strong enough to be in charge in a loving way for the child to learn to trust and bond. A therapist that recommends using "behavior modification techniques" such as star charts does not understand Attachment Disorder! Traditional therapies are not recommended as they have proven to be ineffective with children who have attachment problems until the broken bond is healed.

<u>How can you tell if a therapist is good?</u> If you meet the therapist and explain that your child has a problem with attachment and lying, and the therapist then takes the child with them, leaving you out of the session-fire the therapist and look for one that listens! Obviously, with the lying child having a captive audience, and no one present who knows the truth, they are in a perfect position to manipulate! Being able to manipulate adults makes these children sicker. The therapist should be strong and confrontive. They must not accept any conning, manipulating or superficial charm from the child. The disturbed child is never put in control of the therapy! The purpose of therapy is to help the child

face their issues and to reconnect the mother and the child. It should take about one month per year of age for your child to heal. (Cline 89) If you have a nine year old child that has been in therapy for two years and is not significantly better you might want to take a look at other therapy options! It is not fair to have your child lose all the joy of childhood battling the rage within their hearts due to inadequate therapy.

One of the worst forms of therapy for Attachment Disorder, ADHD or Tourette Syndrome children is time. Waiting for them to outgrow the behaviors DOES NOT WORK. These conditions, left uncontrolled, can destroy a child or turn them into a killer, a rapist, a child abuser or a suicide statistic. Each passing year wears the parents down more and the child becomes sicker, more destructive, and BIGGER! DO NOT WAIT! Get effective help now, and start using these parenting tools right away!

Wesley age 12, still healing from ADHD and RAD, shares his thoughts on therapy from one who's "been there, done that", for parents who want help for their child:

> My first therapist was a very soft, gentle therapist who didn't really get down to the core. It was talk therapy. She got to nothing. Every time she thought we were making progress, I was just manipulating her. I was just lying and manipulating. Manipulating: like lying, fake crying, try to say what she wanted to hear. She didn't know I was fake crying because I was really good at it! I talked and played, and it didn't help me. People thought I was making progress, but I wasn't because she wasn't tough enough for me. Tough therapists don't take garbage. Garbage: lying, manipulating. I went to her for a year or so. She didn't help me because I still got suspended from school and wasn't doing well. I would lie in a continuous cycle 'Oh, my homework I got done at school'. I would get in trouble in the neighborhood. Stomped and destroyed this kid's fort behind his back. I ended up in a psych hospital because I tried to kill myself. I had two different talk therapists before and after I was in the institution, and I could con both of them equally well.

> My attachment therapist was a tough therapist, she started on my anger, what made me sad and/or mad. I did pretty good during the holidays. I was off and on. I got pretty real with her. I got real with this therapist because I knew I couldn't manipulate her, because when I tried, she'd call me on it in my face. In the beginning I was in a new neighborhood, and was at the bus stop with the new kids

and one little one messed with me so I pushed the kid down. I kept pushing this kid down; every time he would get up, I kept pushing him down. I got suspended. I had learned not to trust anybody at all. I kind-of trusted my therapist because she knew what was up, sort-of. I was good at getting people to feel sorry for me. I could go for a few weeks being good.

I think this holding therapist knows me too well. I did try to con her, but it didn't work. When I tested her and it didn't work, I thought , 'Oh shit! I'm not going to be able to con her, what am I going to do? She's going to make me get all the bad and mad out'. I kind of like my mad, because I feel it makes me powerful. But, I do know that it's not powerful because I lost my family and many friends over it. Then I figured I guess I should try or make an effort, otherwise my legs would fall off from having to kick so long in the session. But I was the one who judged how long I had to kick. I'm real about 1/3 of the time. I don't know what love is or how it feels like, but I can sort of remember what it was like when I was a little kid. It was the ultimate feeling.

Don't let the kids fool you! I feel if I didn't have a powerful attachment therapist I probably would have turned into a mass murderer or a serial killer. I wouldn't have a family and I would be locked up into a mental institution, and would have probably killed myself. I feel I can still be fixed because I haven't killed yet.

There is hope for this child, just as there is for every child. No matter what they have already done, or had done to them, if there is one person who cares enough to commit to being a full-time part of their life and give them tight structure and powerful nurturing, they can heal.

PART II

POWERFUL PARENTING TECHNIQUES

THE DYNAMIC DOZEN

IF I can stop one heart from breaking,
I shall not live in vain;
If I can ease one Life the Aching ,
or Cool one pain,
Or help one fainting Robin
Unto his Nest again,
I shall not live in vain.

Emily Dickinson

We are going to examine twelve parenting techniques that will help you take control and give your child an opportunity to heal. All techniques are equally important, and to succeed, must all be used. These techniques, if followed in a loving manner, will result in your interacting with your child in a positive, constructive way. In time, approximately one month for every year your child has lived, your child should respond positively. This is not the time to wait. This is the time to teach, guide and nurture your child with powerful parenting!

PRELIMINARY GUIDELINES

Because each child and each circumstance is different, the techniques are general. There can be no long list of "do's and don'ts" that would fit every situation. The specific actions you take must be of your own creation.

The twelve techniques are not a check list to be used one after another. Instead, *all twelve must be used simultaneously*, as part of a unified plan to be most effective. However, it may be easier to start with number one and add the next technique as soon as you are competent with the previous ones. They are listed in the order of implementation to ensure the greatest level of success. I recommend that you read the entire book before you begin and then re-read each chapter as you prepare to begin the techniques. Some parents have begun all of the new methods as quickly as two weeks! Some have taken twelve weeks, adding one new technique per week while continuing those previously started. I suggest if you do one new tool per week, review the previous chapter to grade yourself before progressing. It is vital to do them in order to avoid wasted effort.

A child with Attachment Disorder will need one full time parent, focused on bonding, for a minimum of six months in order to have the best chance of success. The first six months of healing is the most intense bonding time when the mother and child should not be separated, except to rest.

Remember:
* You control the smiles and the hugs . The disturbed child does not.
* Work from your head, not your heart.
* It is better to start too strict and lighten up, than the reverse.
* Be consistent with rules and expectations/vary the consequences
* Stay focused on the goal (to have a loveable child and a happy home)
* Underneath the monster is a hurting child. That's the one you are fighting for (not with!) That's the one you snuggle, hold and love forever.

POWERFUL PARENTING TECHNIQUES-THE DYNAMIC DOZEN

1. Take care of yourself first

2. Establish respect

3. Create and maintain a heart to heart connection

4. Teach self control

5. Set Limits - Help your child accept limits

6. Supercharge your expectations of responsibility

7. Expect restitution for damages

8. Remove barriers between you and your child

9. Avoid the wrong battles and win the war against rage

10. Teach your child to think for him/herself

11. Guide the processing of feelings

12. Build self esteem

CHAPTER ONE: TAKE CARE OF YOURSELF FIRST

He that can take rest is greater than he that can take cities.
Benjamin Franklin

Taking care of yourself is akin to having a designated driver. Just as you would not choose a drunk driver in control of your car, it is equally unwise to chose to be an exhausted, irritated, or over stressed parent in charge of your child. The mirror image reflected in the mother's eyes echoes to the child, "You're okay", "I love you!" or "Go away, don't bother me any more." The smile in a mother's eyes, repeatedly reassuring the child of his worth, is an invaluable tool in building self esteem. The simple wordless statement through the eyes of love and acceptance needs to be repeated at different intervals depending on the severity of the child's illness. Some children require bonding geared attention as often as every two minutes throughout the day, daily. This can be a serious wipe-out! So what is the solution?

Take some time off to do something that you enjoy to recharge your energy at least once a week. Try: a simple bubble bath to soak away your cares, a drive, bowling, taking a class, movies, dinner, shopping or a trip to a museum. Develop a hobby such as painting, quilting, jogging, bicycling, crafts, riding horses, or belly button fuzz collecting. When you are on an airplane, the instructions are to cover your own mouth when the oxygen masks drop, before assisting a child with their mask. This is the same way with life. Your basic needs must be met before you will have the strength and patience to meet the child's needs. If you're driven over the edge, if you are exhausted and can no longer function rationally, who will take care of your child?

Sleep - you need to get caught up (10 - 12 hours, first few weeks). If you are a two parent family, stagger your sleep time. A normal adult needs 8 hours.

Put an alarm on your child's bedroom door (and window if necessary). These can be purchased at stores selling electronic gear or through a locksmith. This is also an important early step in regaining control of your home and establishing authority. You need to be able to sleep soundly at night. Disturbed children should NEVER share a room with another child! *Sexually abused children will often continue to act out sexually if not stopped!* Carnal knowledge does not just go away. You must protect your child from hurting other children and pets and injuring their healing heart in the process.   Children that have been abused physically or sexually feel safer with an alarm . These children are most afraid at night because that's usually when the abuse took place. They can't sleep because of fear and are often up wandering around their rooms for hours. They sometimes sleep on the floor rather than the bed because of too many bad memories. An alarm helps them feel safer because no one can get in without setting it off and they cannot get out to get themselves in trouble. They are safer both ways, and so are you!

Have a portable alarm if they spend the night at Grandma's or somewhere else. Anytime, anywhere, children with Attachment Disorder must have an alarm at night. We have had children who can sleep one or two hours a night. One 9 year old girl, nicknamed t-bear, as her family was sleeping, would wander the house at night, hacking up stairs, furniture and panelling, preparing to hack up her newly adopted mom! I've had several moms tell me of awakening to find a gruesome drawing (blood dripping knives, etc.) as a warning from their child. We had one nine year old boy, Michael, that molested thirteen neighborhood children at night while his parents thought he was sleeping! The alarm is used for at least a year, every night. It is not a punishment to be turned off and on. The child is not given permission to open their door, which sets the alarm off, unless it is a real emergency or the child is ill. The parents must open the child's bedroom door rather than allow the child to do it until the alarm is no longer needed. Having it removed or turned off is a priviledge that is earned through hard work and honest effort.

Proper nutrition and vitamins. The emotional stress you are under requires extra B vitamins and calcium for your nerves. Plan easy meals and snacks like fresh fruit, especially bananas, yogurt, hard boiled eggs, cottage cheese, etc.

You need time for quiet every day. Discover your "think within spot" where you go to nurture yourself. A spot in the yard, attic, bedroom. Take time out and time away. Go on walks, talk with your spouse, exercise or jog, listen to music. Mozart's music has proven to be very therapeutic. Consider the use of a walkman to "tune out" outside noises, such as screaming fits and obscenities hurled in your face. Police officers use great ear protectors on the shooting range that could give your ears a rest. One of our rules is: no one bothers mom in the bathroom unless there is blood or fire.

Take care of your nervous system. Be aware of the accumulative effects of stress. Write a list of your own needs. Be sure to include time off for fun. When you feel an emotional drain coming on, take care of it immediately. Offer your child an option by saying, "I feel an energy drain coming on. Would you like to do an extra chore for me to help me out or spend 30 minutes of quiet time in your room to give me a coffee break?" Use your free time to put your feet up, listen to your favorite, uplifting music, have hot cocoa or lemonade; rest your spirit, completely guilt free, at least once every day.

Call in the reserves at the onset of weariness rather than wait until total exhaustion causes you to lose control. Some moms feel guilty admitting their limitations. Be strong enough to accept yourself as human-not flawless. Guilt and worry are very draining and counter-productive. Be wary of channeling your energy into guilt or worry. Be conscious of channeling that energy into growth and life. Hire and train someone to take your child for the day or weekend at least once a month! (See appendix G for training brochure to copy and use) We also have a great video called Give Me a Break! It teaches how to find and train relief.

Taking care of the couple relationship is vital for your success as a couple as well as important modeling for the children to see . Your spouse can be an excellent source of renewal. Set a date night and have some fun with your spouse. Do not discuss the child! Listen to each other. Laugh together.

Buy a book or go to the library. The Chicken Soup for the Soul series is inspiring, uplifting and in short sections. Perfect for enjoying yourself when the child is attempting to make you angry and thus prove their power. Smile. You win! Another great book is 99 Ways to Drive Your Child Sane. It is a hoot! You can order it on the last page of this book.

Test yourself for Post Traumatic Stress Disorder and Depression.(See Appendixes C, D, + E). If you test positive, GET HELP NOW. Learn to know yourself. It's important to recognize your own limitations and tolerance levels. Learn to walk away before you become too tired to be effective with your child. Develop the ability to say "I'm sorry, I blew it." Being honest about your humanness models for your child how they should take care of their emotional welfare. Parents of these difficult children can benefit from therapy a great deal. Locating a therapist who understands you and supports you can be a life saver. Call a therapist and your family doctor. To find a therapist, ask friends and family members for recommendations. When the same name comes up twice, call them and make an appointment!

Establish a support system of people, who understand, to call and process your thoughts, vent your rage and have respite care. Make a list of 10 people right now. Call them and ask if they will be on your support team for the next 6 months to 1 year. Calls are limited to 10 minutes. Children should not be able to hear you! DO NOT ALLOW YOURSELF TO BECOME ISOLATED OR FORCED OVER THE EDGE . These kids can often push parents past their limit of patience and over the edge. Pain does not aid healing or "teach them a lesson". It does not increase bonding. The mom of a child with attachment problems, ADD, ADHD, or Tourette Syndrome needs twelve hugs a day to survive.

IDENTIFY YOUR POWER DRAINS AND ELIMINATE THEM

Understand that ONE straw broke the camel's back and prevent it from happening to you. Give consequences to unacceptable behavior THE FIRST TIME. It takes much less energy to correct the problem in the beginning than to tolerate it to the point of exhaustion for years. Why not start today and teach your child to overcome their behavior problems and use your energy tomorrow for something a lot more fun!

When Love Is Not Enough

Eliminate problems such as:

Useless chatter (jabbering)-Have them put their hand over their mouth for a minute or two until they gain control! No explanation, just action.

Whining-have them take a nap immediately. Tired toddlers whine to let adults know they need rest. Powerful parents provide it swiftly with love and understanding. If they whine on the way to their nap add another 15-30 minutes! Thank them for letting you know how tired they are! This works for all ages.

Interrupting-is a signal to the powerful parent that the child needs help practicing being patient. Two to five minutes of strong sitting is usually practice enough. Then, of course, ask the little interrupter what was so important and give them your full attention and a hug.

Pity parties- (The poor starved basset hound look) Sometimes a child does not realize how blessed they are to have loving parents, good food, and a nice warm bed. They prefer to elicit sadness and pity from friends, neighbors, siblings and strangers. They need appreciation training! I recommend they go to a trained respite home where they can work for everything just like an adult has to do. Minimum effort provides soup kitchen rewards. Maximum effort provides a trip home! You may have to train your own respite provider, Feel free to copy the brochure for respite care on pages 96 - 97. Another quick elimination of pity parties is to put sunglasses on your basset hound. Mickey Mouse ones are best!

Bedtime hassles-7:00 for young kids (they need 10 to 12 hours of sleep when they are growing) 7:30 for older kids (they need homework time). Many parents have curfew times for children to be in their rooms early enough for parents to have uninterrupted time together. Time to share and dream with your partner can be very encouraging and help restore your sanity. Strategic planning sessions held often can be great morale boosters in the war against whining and rejection. Just as young lovers use the five parts of bonding, eye contact, touch, movement, smiles, and sugar, so should you and your spouse to help maintain your closeness.

How do you get them to bed without a war? out of their room past bed time, NO reminders from parents!! This is a great opportunity to teach punctuality! Consequence for draining your energy or taking your time away from spouse is to give back time--one extra chore for every minute the child is late to bed. After he is up ten to twenty minutes late, calmly ask, "Did I remember to tell you that you owe one free chore for every minute you are up late?" Bedtime means in their room and quiet. They get in bed and turn out the light when they feel tired, whatever hour that may be. NO parental interference. YOU cannot make them go to sleep. Don't try. You will lose! Let them learn to listen to their bodies and put themselves to sleep when it is needed. This is good to learn before they go off to college! They should be good at it by 5 or 6 years old. Before that they often need to be tucked in with a bedtime ritual (bath, reading, or back rub, etc.) New research has shown that light around us when we are sleeping keeps us from going into a deep enough sleep. The light from night lights, street lights or even moonlight shining in the window must be eliminated. If your child sleeps with the light on just take the light bulb and have them earn it back after a few days.

Television-get rid of it, cut off the plug, or lock it in the closet. A child with ADD, or ADHD cannot have "brain shut down time" by doing passive activities such as TV, video or computer games. They must remain active, interacting, problem solving, feeling, touching, being alive. Staring into an electronic box sets them back, not forward!! I have them away from these things for a year or more until their mind is healed and can focus and problem solve on a normal level.

Establish a proactive solution to triangulation between yourselves and the other significant adults that relate to your child; therapists, spouses, teachers, church members, extended family and friends.Triangulation is setting one adult against the other by acting differently to each. For example, the child might act pitiful to one and aggressive toward the other in order to have the adults split rather than function as a team. Divorce rate is very high in families with these children. These children have a high incidence of false allegations of abuse. Be ready BEFORE this type of devastating event may impact your family. Have a signed paper declaring this child has a history of reporting false abuse incidents. Talk to teachers before the child attends school or Sunday School.

PREPARING AND SETTING UP YOUR HOME

Wouldn't you puppy-proof or child-proof before a puppy or a toddler arrives to keep them safe? It is important in the beginning to prepare your home before you begin, rather than be sorry later. These changes are only necessary until your child is healed. They are designed to make your life less stressful by avoiding unpleasant situations. I am speaking from experience. I remember clearly finding out, *after* I used my toothbrush, that a child had used it to clean the toilet!

Establish a lock-up area. This is an area - a locked closet, rental unit or bank deposit box - that is locked and only you and your partner (if you have one) have the key. It must be large enough to keep items that your child is not to have access to without your permission. A hardware store should have the necessary items for less than $20. Put in this area all dangerous items and other things to which your child is to have no access. Especially dangerous items, such as guns, should be double locked (for kids under 6 years old), and triple locked (for kids ages 6-20 years). Sporting goods stores sell inexpensive trigger locks. Other items to be stored in lock up: prescription drugs, household chemicals (e.g. chlorine cleaners), hunting knives, dangerous tools (e.g. hammers), money, car keys, documents, credit cards, baseball bats, golf clubs, matches, hockey sticks, bows and arrows, trophies/awards, jewelry, heirlooms, coin collections, etc. A lockable desk can protect expensive computer equipment.

Put all your personal supplies, tooth brush, hair care items, shampoo, make- up, razor in a portable case for transport. DO NOT leave the items you need to take care of yourself in the path of a destructive child.

Protect your pets-relocate fish tanks/bird cages to an off limit area. Develop a plan to protect your dog or cat or their food and water from ever being alone or unprotected with a child with attachment problems. All living things need protection. If your child can injure or kill another living being, the damage to your child will be great. Be aware of this potential in any child with RAD.

You can take two approaches of working with your child: 1. Learn the theories and philosophy of Attachment Disorder and then begin the parenting techniques outlined in this manual, or 2. Begin with the template instructions in Appendix A, and learn theories and philosophy as you go.

With children, time is crucial. The younger the child the easier and quicker it is to obtain results. The sooner you can regain control, the sooner healing for your child and your family begins.

CHAPTER TWO: <u>ESTABLISH RESPECT</u>

Men are respectable only as they respect.
Ralph Waldo Emerson

There's an old book on parenting where the father is in charge of the children, as fathers traditionally were before the year 1830. (Blankenhorn 1995) In this book the children break the rules, and the father punishes them with fire and brimstone. They break the rules some more, and he punishes them by grounding them. We are talking some major grounding here. They were grounded for forty years in the desert. They still broke the rules, didn't appreciate him, and complained all the time. Then he demonstrated a powerful parenting technique that works well. He said, "I'm out of here! When you get your act together, do things my way, and are fun to be around, you can join me. I love you very much, and I'll have a special place waiting for you." This is from a great book, I highly recommend. It's called <u>The Bible</u>! In this book the translation says we are supposed to "fear" The Father. I always had a hard time with that, so I checked with a biblical scholar, who shared with me that the original word is "Yarra". "Yarra" is a Greek word meaning "to hold in awe". It is essential that your child "holds you in awe". We are awesome!

Bowlby's definition of attachment is " an affectional tie with some other differentiated and preferred individual who is usually conceived as stronger and/or wiser." (Bowlby 1977a) So, here you see, it is essential that the children hold a powerful parent in awe in order to bond. If Mom comes across as ignorant because she is in denial about the child's behavior, the child will not heal. If she appears uncaring because she's too tired to try to stop the child, the child will not heal. If she appears out of control because the child can "make her angry", Mom and child both lose because she is showing weak character. If she is inept because she doesn't know what to do with the child, the child with attachment problems will not heal.

The title of "Mom" is a title of honor just above Queen. The title of "Dad" is a title of honor just above King. As royalty your children beneath you are then the prince and/ or princess. If you are the doormat who lies down and lets the child walk all over you, then because your child is beneath you, they are the dirt under the door mat. You must claim your title as Mom or Dad and from this day forward expect the respect you deserve. No longer allow your subjects to treat you as mere mortals. You deserve to be treated with honor and respect because you hug the unhuggable, love the unlovable and have opened your hearts and your home to a child that gives little or nothing in return. Here you are reading this book, looking for more answers because you are an awesome, awesome parent! I salute you! You deserve to be treated with great honor. Insist on nothing less.

How do you start making positive, powerful changes in your home and in your relationship with your child? You begin with your eyes meeting theirs. You deserve the respect of eye contact when speaking with anyone. What you or they have to say deserves full attention.

ESTABLISHING RESPECT THROUGH EYE CONTACT

"Eye Contact" is not just looking at your child. It is the reaching into their soul with your eyes - rested, loving, powerful eyes that say to your child, "You're okay. You have me. You're lucky." This telegraphs into the child's mind as, "I'm Okay." You will reinforce this message to your child over and over, throughout the day, throughout life.

Eye contact is POWERFUL - even very brief eye contact. Eye contact is an expression of love as well as a weapon. You must be very conscious of how you are using eye contact. Keep it soft and loving. One brief look of daggers from your eyes can undo weeks of work. I had one mom who trained her child not to make eye contact by saying, "Look at Me!" and then chewed him out with anger in her eyes. Use action, not anger!

If you are tired, exhausted, or angry and look into your child's eyes, the message you send is "What am I going to do with you?" Your child will think, "Mom doesn't know what she's doing. I have the power."

When you speak to your child, the child must always make eye contact with you when listening and answering. If this is a problem for your child, it's a great opportunity for practice! You could choose to wait silently and complete your sentence when the child looks up. You could assist the child with the oxygen supply to their brain by having them do ten (no more than ten) push-ups or jumping jacks in order to increase their circulation and help their focus. Be sure you are assisting them by making it easy to look into your eyes because of the love you hold there. If you expect a child to maintain eye contact when you have lost control and are angry, you are undoing the work you are trying to accomplish. You are demolishing the bond.

When you call your child, the child must always come to you and make eye contact when listening to you. A fun time to practice this is fifteen or twenty minutes before the child wants to be some place, such as a friend's house, soccer game, etc. Announce to the child recall practice will begin. Seat yourself in a comfortable chair and tell the child to go to their room and expect a call. When they get there sweetly say "Ethel, come here!". When the child arrives in your presence congratulate them on making it the entire distance! Have them return to their room with the directions to return when called, make eye contact, and say "Yes, Mom!" with enthusiasm and respect. Practice until they do it exactly right your way. Use all positive reinforcement, lots of pizzazz, and lots of loving eye contact and hugs. This practice can be done whenever it is convenient for you and not necessarily at the moment the child needs correction.

When your child speaks to you, expect the respect of eye contact before anything is said. Turn the radio or any distracting noise off. Meet their eyes with a smile in your eyes. They do not yell your name from another room. They should respect you enough to locate you visually and then speak. This can be practiced with a rousing game of hide and speak. You hide and the child must locate you visually and says "Mom!" or "Dad!". This always ends with a big hug.

When you reply to your child, your eye contact is very important. Do not be distracted with other work while discussing anything.

Your position is important. It is much more powerful to have your munchkin physically looking up at you rather than you being in a lower position. Normal children, when they are hurt or fearful are met with a loving adult kneeling down to their level and comforting them. Children with attachment problems are not comforted by an adult "coming down to their level". They feel safer when the adult comes from a position of power and it's not on their knees (unless they are in prayer!) If you are sitting in a chair have the child sit next to you on the floor or you stand up. When hugging the child stand up straight and strong! The reason for this is to have a strong adult to bond to and so the child feels safer (Not intimidated!).

ESTABLISH RESPECT THROUGH SPEECH PATTERNS

You have your position correct. Your eye contact is soft and filled with belief and love. Now, how do you talk? What do you say? I was once in a shoe store, selecting a purchase when I heard a typical American interaction between mother and child. It went like this: "Joey, come here! I found some great shoes for you!" said the loving Mom. The swift curt reply "What!! I'm looking over here!" was met with a wimpy "okay" from Mom. She patiently waited and then purchased the shoes he selected. He was about 8 years old, in control of a doormat Mom. A correct response would have been to return to his side, take his hand, and leave the store with no explanation. These kids learn from action, NOT from listening. They seek negative attention, so we don't use it!!

The child should hear what you say the first time. Disturbed children play a little power game called wear-out the folks with questions and reruns. Powerful parents do not repeat themselves. If the child needs more oxygen to get their brain in gear, 10 or 15 excellent A+ jumping jacks or pushups usually does the trick. Then ask, "What did I just say?" If they still don't know have them do another 10 or 15 to be sure their brain is engaged before repeating yourself. Your time is valuable and what you have to say is important, so be sure the child is ready to listen. Listening exercises are also helpful. Just whisper something several times throughout the day when your child is nearby such as, "Do you want some candy ?" . When they answer, congratulate them on their excellent hearing and enjoy the candy or ice cream together! Let them know how lucky they are to have such an awesome parent to give them listening practice so they can get over having weak ears!

The correct response is "Yes, Mom" or "No, Mom" (or Dad). It is acceptable for them to reply, "I don't want to, but I will do it anyway". This is being honest. It is unacceptable for the child to respond with grunts, shrugs, incomplete words or phrases (yeah) or non-words (unhuh), or "I don't know" when dealing with feelings.The words "I can't" in a child with attachment problems means, "I won't"!

When given directions it is unacceptable for the child to ask "why?" or "what?". NEVER answer these questions. There is no need for you to defend your position. Getting in a debate with the child erodes your power, challenges your authority, and validates the child's pathological sense of importance. Remember, have a consequence ready when a rule is challenged. If your child whines, "Why do I have to?", calmly reply, "That is a good question! After you finish doing what I just asked you to do, you will sit down and write an answer to ' why I would want you to do this'." You say this without anger and while keeping warm eye contact (hold a beautiful thought about something positive about the child to keep your eyes filled with love). The discussion is over. Keep all interactions to two sentences or less. That is all the information they are able to soak up in the beginning.

"Please" and "thank you" require special attention, both by you and your child. YOU use "please" when asking the child to do something for you personally, such as, "Please get me..." If you are TELLING the child to do something for themselves or the family, DO NOT USE "PLEASE." You will say "I want you to clean your room. Got it?" You do NOT say, "Will you please clean your room? Okay?" Asking "okay?" is asking their permission. Make it clear it is a direction, not a request! Their reply ,"Okay", is saying 'it's okay with them if they do what you said'. It is not nearly as respectful as "Yes, Mom!"

When asking for things such as for water or bathroom use, (YES! They have to ask!!!) the correct request is, "May I please have a drink?" or "May I please use the bathroom?" The use of complaints for action on your part must be eliminated. " I have to go to the bathroom really bad" is not even close to respectful communication. If you allow them to treat royalty (that's YOU!), in their home, in this manner, how much less respect will teachers and other authority figures get? It all starts with their relationship with you and ripples out like on a clear pond into the rest of the world. "Yes, ma'am." or "Yes, sir." is used with non-family members such as teachers. Having a child say, "Yes ma'am" to their Mom is too distant and not as connecting. It makes children feel unwanted and unaccepted.

The use of "we" can be a problem. Do not use "we" as in, "We are going to be nice today, aren't we?" Aligning with their misbehavior weakens your position. My favorite memory involving the misuse of the word "we" occurred when I took an 8 year old to stay overnight at a "trained" respite provider's home. This young blue-eyed charmer had beaten her family's two Rottweilers to death with a baseball bat, poisoned her grandmother's two Cocker Spaniels with her ritalin, and pulled the wings off a bird to watch it die. A tough case, she was wearing me out, so in taking good care of myself (technique #1), I was taking some time off. The "trained" Mom bent down to this little girl and said, "Now, we aren't going to pee in our room, are we? Because if we do pee on our room, we are going to sleep in the bathtub! You got that!" The little raven-haired cutie looked as amazed as I was. I was standing there trying to visualize the two of them....! What a thought! Be careful with that one!

Try adding a new respectful behavior each day or every other day while maintaining the ones you have already established. This makes it less overwhelming to remember everything. Once you get this piece on track, you are really rolling. Are they going to be happy you have accepted your throne? NO WAY! *They* want it! Disturbed children have no intention of treating you with respect. To do so they have to admit you are above them and worthy of their honor. It is a battle well worth fighting! When you win, so does your child and the rest of society. Establish the eye contact and speech patterns of respect as soon as you are rested and ready for the fight for your child's emotional life to begin! Remember, you must enforce them consistently. Have a consequence ready when the rule is challenged, and a loving encouragement when the rule is complied with. *Catch them doing it right!!*

ESTABLISH RESPECT THROUGH MANNERS

You should require your child to be well mannered and polite. Manners were designed to help us live together in a society without infringing on each other's space or irritating each other. It is about being considerate and thoughtful. If the emotionally disturbed child has been given the power in the family be prepared to have a serious battle on your hands as you fight to set your child's heart back on track and regain your family's peace.

No discussion! A family is not a democracy where everyone votes, otherwise we would eat ice cream at every meal and live at Disneyland. The adults may ask for opinions from healthy members of the group before making a final decision.

Being helpful and thoughtful should begin before your child reaches the age of five. He should be expected to open doors and carry packages for parents.

Walking is done next to, NOT in front of, the adult. It makes the kid feel like they are leading the pack when they go through doorways first or lead the way. I usually begin by holding the child's hand until they are either over the age of 4 or stable enough to stay next to me. These children have major leadership issues due to their lack of trust. I do, however, recommend they be given permission to walk in front going up and down stairs. It is very easy to grab an adult leg and yank to create a disaster. I once had a unique child we nick-named Picasso (because he was incredibly creative). He went to hike up the mountain with a less disturbed child. Walking behind the other child, dear little Picasso whipped out his penis and sprayed down the back of the other boy. I was very impressed with the restraint the older boy showed as he returned Picasso alive!

Eating with nice manners is a common problem for children with attachment problems. Even though they have been taught lovingly many times and lectured and scolded they continue to eat "gross" at family meals. Gulping, slurping, and talking with a mouth very full of partially chewed food, using fingers to push food onto eating utensils, and food all over their faces are typical eating patterns for these kids. If it grosses out the folks, they repeat it! If they can cause a scene or battle during family time to sabotage closeness they will! Lovingly and firmly excuse your slurper from the table the first time they do it! They can finish eating by themselves at the picnic table, in the laundry room, or elsewhere. From now on, only the civilized share the meal together. Each meal the whole family is gathered around the table (not the TV), and the games begin! I like to watch how long it takes them to get excused from the table. Each time it usually gets longer and longer; eventually they make it through the entire meal with you! Be sure and celebrate with hugs and pizzazz! Be prepared, for the next night they will most likely test again. But the testing will come less and less often if you pass the test with an A+ each time! The television is not on during meals. This is the time to enjoy your meal, discuss interesting non- threatening topics and make loving eye contact with each other. Those who finish their meal usually have room for dessert. Those who don't of course don't have room. Children are feed meals according to what the parents feel their growing bodies need, not what the child demands. Everyone is entitled to ONE or TWO items they don't care to eat. Respectful children say, "May I please be excused from the table?" and when given permission they clear their place and prepare to help clean the kitchen.

Phone manners are important, Children should not answer the phone (or door) until they are old enough to take efficient messages and handle whatever may occur (obscene phone calls, solicitors, people wanting information that is none of their business, etc.). Answering the phone gives the child power. Be sure they have earned the privilege first! When an adult is on the phone, the children should be considerate and keep the noise down. If they need help with that I like to have the ring of the phone be the signal for them to run to their "think-within-spot" (see Chapter 4) and remain until the conversation is over. Of course, conversations should be kept under 10 minutes. If they need even more practice, have them sit when you ring a bell.

Respect for property such as feet on furniture, feet on the car seats, or tipping chairs is taught by simply having the abuser stand for the rest of the meal or the rest of the day. Sometimes I have them sit on the floor. No explanation. They know what they did. You have probably told them a hundred times. No more! For rudeness such as walking on the grass instead of using the sidewalk, I like to put them in charge of part of the lawn care at home or where they walked on the grass to help them learn how much work is involved. Parents need to model respect for each other, for authority, police, and laws . We must model obeying laws we don't like such as: speed limits, dog leash laws, picking up feces your dog leaves off your property. We set an example by doing it right whether we like it or not!

Car manners are critical because they affect safety. Car travel can be a control issue and a power drain, BE READY. When it becomes a dangerous situation the distraction needs to be dealt with to ensure the safety of the rest of the occupants. The driver needs to halt the vehicle immediately! Do not wait until foam is coming from your clenched teeth! A mature enough child in good weather might need to walk home. It is safest to follow at a distance in the car. Or the child could do push-ups on the side of the road until the specified amount is done correctly. This only works if you have a very loose time schedule. Both hands on top of the head for a short while keeps busy hands out of trouble.
*Seat belts on - immediately - and stay on.
*The child does not talk in the car unless you (or another adult) speak to the child and expect an answer. If your authority is challenged, the child holds one hand over their mouth. Challenged again, two hands over the mouth. A third time, the child puts their forehead on their knees. An additional challenge, pull over and stop the car. Go home if necessary. You must triumph as the authority . When you win the child wins, when you lose you both lose.

*The adult controls the radio. The child may listen to their selection of music on their own radio, in their own space. In your car you listen to what will help you be a safer driver.
* The air temperature and window position is selected by the driver. A polite request for more heat or air from the munchkin crew of course will be taken into account by a loving parent.

Be creative, catch them off guard so they are busy trying to figure out what you are up to, rather than the reverse. Some creative ideas from some AWESOME MOMS:

Paula Barney-rented a port-a-potty for her RAD child who could not handle using the family bathroom without causing major problems. Guess who pays for it!

Sharon Ramsay-left her kids, who had been acting obnoxious, with a relief mom for the day with a chore list. The secret list said, "Have a cup of hot cocoa, make a snowman, sled for 30 minutes, have cookies and milk before lunch, etc. Each "chore" was a loving gift from mom! She was pounced on and hugged when she returned!

Helen Bandarra- Every time her son threw a fit, she got a day off! He went to respite.

Marlene Bloome-Went on vacation and took a nanny! The nanny watched the child during the day and the nanny had evenings off to see the sights. Everyone won!

The Wainwrights- Had their daughter not only pay her court costs but also her attorney fees when she was arrested for stealing. She is 12 years old!

One Awesome family from Colorado had their child pay THEIR attorney fees when she made false allegations against them!

Sheila Mckaim hid a video camera in the laundry basket she carried into the child's room when she asked him to read something for her. She showed the school the film. They finally believed her! He had them convinced he couldn't!

CHAPTER THREE: <u>CREATE AND MAINTAIN A HEART TO HEART CONNECTION</u>

Kind Words can be short and easy to speak, but
their echoes are truly endless.   Mother Teresa

Taking care of yourself and establishing respect are some of the things that need to be done before your child will be ready to open their heart to you. You must be rested, loving and in charge before any bonding can occur with a child who has bonding problems. To connect to your child, you must meet all of your child's basic needs. Everyday your child needs:

*balanced nutrition
*clothing
*sunshine,
*bed and blankets
*play time
*medical care
*exercise
*boundaries
*chores
*unconditional love
*bonding (eye contact, touch, movement, smiles, sugar)

To be emotionally stable, children need to give and receive affection. Kids with attachment problems do not want affection. Their experience with affection has been painful, so they avoid close relationships. That is an understatement! They not only avoid relationships, they put every effort into sabotaging them. They actually prefer to be hated to being loved! To overcome their defenses, you must use clear, concise nurturning techniques.

The following emotional bonding tools must be used together daily. This is their "heart medication" to heal the damage to their emotional heart. You as the emotionally stable parent are responsible to provide this necessary medication. The child will attempt to undermine your efforts because of his intense fear of bonding, pain, and loss. If you allow the disturbed child to be in control and destroy your attempts at snuggle time, you will lose, and your child will lose. It is essential that you remain strong, in charge, and love your child through their tough times. They must be nurtured in a very concrete way, not just when they're cute and snuggly, but when they're angry, defiant, obnoxious and unbathed. They need to know you love them for who they are, not for what they do, how they look, how they smell, or if it fits into your schedule. If your snuggle time becomes less often than needed, beware: the child is in control of the relationship. The necessary input for effective bonding is eye contact, touch, movement, smiles, and sugar (Ainsworth, 1972; Cline, 1979; Cohen, 1974; Masters & Wellman, 1974; Yarrow, 1961, 1964, 1972).

♥ Eye Contact-- must be soft and loving. Every minute you spend looking lovingly into your child's eyes will save you about an hour of pain when they're teenagers. "The eye is the window to the soul." While making eye contact, you are giving your love from your heart through your eyes into your child's eyes and straight into their heart. They will try to avoid it. Be compassionate and firm. They must accept your loving eye contact to heal their heart.

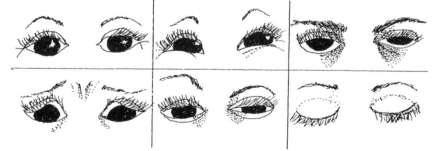

Mom's eyes- the mirror for the child's self image

♥Touch is so vital, humans actually die without it. We, as human beings, need eight hugs a day to maintain emotional stability, We need twelve hugs a day for emotional healing. Normal teenagers need twelve. Teen sex has been defined as "looking for touch in all the wrong places". "The sense most closely associated with the skin, the sense of touch, is the earliest to develop in the human embryo. The communications we transmit through touch constitute the most powerful means of establishing human relationships, the foundation of experience. Where touching begins, there love and humanity also begin - within the first minutes following birth. Learning to learn, learning to love, and to be kind are so closely interconnected and so profoundly interwoven, especially with the sense of touch, it would greatly help toward our rehumanization if we would pay closer attention to the need we all have for tactual experience" (Montague, 1986). These children, so hurt, so untrusting, need to be held. They need to have an arm around their shoulders, a hand squeezed or a cheek caressed. They need your time and your touch. They won't make it easy for you. When you hug them their bodies become rigid. They often scream OW! or dig their chin into your shoulder or body. They need to be taught how to hug. They need to wrap their arms around you, with their arms under your arms, hands flat on your back, not in a wrestling hold. The child does not pat the parent on the back in a role reversal. *Disturbed children are not allowed to ask for hugs.* The child should not be in control of loving interaction! Until the relationship is well healed, it is on the healthy parent's terms only. A loving parent provides lots of hugs. The child must trust that they will.

♥Movement stimulates the part of the brain that helps us to develop, learn to control ourselves and heal our bodies. Hospital studies have shown patients having hospital beds that rock had less secondary infections and more rapid healing. (Rocky Mountain News - Tues. 4/7/92) Some great ways to add movement to your life include: Rocking, it's very relaxing; Dancing, grab your child up in your arms put on some lively music and boogie; Horseback riding, it's been proven to be very therapeutic and helps to curb sexual acting out. Having a horse available for the child to ride (when earned), has proven to be much less expensive than teen pregnancy; Mini-trampolines are excellent for energy release during cold winter days. It stimulates the immune system while helping the limbic system, which is the emotional center of the brain.

♥Smiles-- It gives you a face-lift. It makes you feel better as well as the entire household. It is the smile in your eyes that we all connect with. Children with bonding problems smile by showing their teeth rather than letting the joy come through their heart and shine on their faces. Reciprocal smiles are used to gauge emotional health. Several times throughout the day, usually mealtimes, try bouncing a smile from your eyes into the child's eyes. If the child reflects your smile by bouncing one right back, they are in good shape. If they don't notice or don't respond, therapy should be scheduled as soon as possible. You do not tell this to the child. Just do it and observe. If the child has just been reprimanded or is ill, don't expect reciprocation.

♥Sugar -- Human milk is the sweetest of all milks, it's sweeter than cow's milk, goat's milk, or even mare's milk. We relate sugar and love very closely together. We call our loved ones "sugar, sweety, honey, etc". Infant formulas made with no sugar are not beneficial to bonding. Elliott Blass from Johns Hopkins University found that sugar actually reduces pain. His research showed that newborns cried significantly less during painful procedures such as circumcision and drawing blood when they were fed sugar, than infants that were not given sugar. (Rocky Mountain News- 2/6/91) This is great news for those of us that are chocoholics. Because sugar actually reduces pain. I like to combine milk with sugar for bonding purposes. Sometimes I use warm milk with vanilla and sugar added. Sometimes I use Milk Duds, ice cream or caramels which are made from milk sugar. Sugar is used to reinforce the bonding process. It is not used alone or outside the bonding enviroment. One exception to this rule is the "Kangaroo pouch". This pouch is a fanny pack filled with goodies, from the real mom, for the child to use when away from mom for a period longer than twenty-four hours, such as in respite. The instructions given to the child with the pack are to eat the goodies whenever they are missing their mom, and that mom has put love in each bite especially for the child.

♥♥♥♥ Snuggle time is used to apply the above five tools simultaneously. It is a special time of holding your child in your arms like an infant, in a comfortable rocking chair. Snuggle time is a fun time for you and your child to share nursery rhymes, silly or favorite songs and stories, or just tell jokes or make funny faces. You can share dreams, memories, or just listen to soothing music all snuggled together. When the child eats chewy caramels during this special time it simulates the jaw movement like a nursing infant and is very relaxing and healing. It also keeps them quiet for a bit! Humans clench their teeth and set their jaw in anger. Making them loosen their jaw up by chewing helps them to calm down. Include all the five parts of bonding in your snuggle time to make it very powerful. Snuggle time should be done six days a week in the beginning of your child's healing. Do not schedule this crucial part of healing at a consistent time such as every evening before bed. Vary the time and the day to avoid control battles. The six day a week schedule should be maintained for the first few months and then gradually reduced over the next six months until it is needed infrequently. The 12 daily hugs are not reduced. They must never fade away. They are essential to healing and happiness!

SNUGGLE TIME IS NOT TIME TO HAVE A CAPTIVE AUDIENCE TO REAM OUT OR LECTURE!! IT IS ABOUT LOVE AND LAUGHTER, CLOSENESS AND CUDDLING!

The disturbed child is not put in charge of hugs and snuggle time. These bonding techniques are like heart medication for a child's broken heart. Just as you would not allow them to decide amounts, type, and how often other medications should be taken, you *must not allow* them to ask for, or demand hugs and snuggle time. You, the emotionally healthy one, decide when the child needs a hug. *Their* behavior does not dictate yours. You don't give heart medication only during heart attacks! You don't give hugs only when they are huggable. They get huggable because you hug them. They get snuggly because you snuggle them.

Note: if the child has sexual problems they need MORE hugs, not LESS!

PIZAZZ (no, not pizza!)

Paying the pizazz paycheck is an art requiring great skill. Pizazz is intense excitement - a raising of voice, a change of tone, wide eyed- eye contact, and an animated expression usually done in staccato interspersed with long who-o-o-o-o-ops of excitement! The craving for pizazz is intense in most children. This craving is so intense, emotionally disturbed children have been known to leap in the path of an oncoming vehicle in order to get pizazz. Difficult children are adept at training unskilled parents to pay them with negative pizazz such as the following scenario: Caseydios has accumulated layers of orange and yellow slime on his teeth. Mom, holding her breath, replies, "Wow! That's really gross! How can you stand it! You probably have the grossest teeth in town! The dog's teeth are cleaner! Your breath smells worse than the sewer!" Several days later the child "accidently" brushes his teeth. Mom responds, "Oh, that's nice. It's about time," Looking at this case, where was the excitement placed? Where did the child get the most exhilaration? The behavior receiving the most pizazz is the one the child will repeat. To put the pizazz correctly in this situation, the yellow slime would be met with, "Honey, there's enough food on your teeth to last you until lunch time." Several days later, the white smile appears. The mother, clutching her breast, literally falls over on the sofa, fanning her face in disbelief, looks at the child and says, "I was struck by the intense gleam coming from your mouth! I was momentarily blinded by the bright shine! Help me up. Let me take a closer look! Holy cow! I thought you were some movie star!" In this case the pizazz and excitement is placed on the desired behavior to encourage repetition. Positive pizazz is used for all well done chores, and respectful, responsible, and fun to be around behavior. *Do not place pizazz on behaviors unless you want them repeated.* Pizazzing properly is one of the essential keys to success. Enjoy it, it's fun!

TALK LESS!
HUG MORE!

CHAPTER FOUR : <u>TEACH SELF-CONTROL</u>

My doctors told me I would never walk again.
My mother told me I would, I believed my mother.
Wilma Rudolph, the first runner ever to win
three gold medals in the same Olympic games

Further progress on any level is impossible if your child has not first learned self-control. Do not attempt to have the child handle any chores or privileges until he has good self control when mad, sad, glad, or scared. It is vital that he have control of himself first!

*<u>The basic tool used to teach self control is POWER SITTING</u>. "Power sitting" means STRONG SITTING. The child is in his "think within spot". You select the spot according to visibility, convenience, safety, distractions, and destructibility. A special chair strategically located is used for children under four. A spot on the floor with a small washable, rubber backed rug for children over four is best.

*Body posture is correct. The correct position is with legs folded, hands folded, BACK STRAIGHT, head straight nothing moving especially the mouth. Facing a blank wall is easiest especially for children with ADD/ADHD (No wallpaper!).

*Start with 1 to 5 consecutive minutes of strong sitting. Build up to one minute per year of life. If the child has ADD or ADHD then the time should be doubled. No more than 20 minutes! Be very aware of distracting noises in the beginning with children with ADD/ADHD. Avoid having the dishwasher, laundry, radio, etc. distracting them. As they get stronger, add these things one at a time to help them develop their skills. This is crucial if you expect the child to function in a classroom. How do you tell if your child really has a genetic attention problem? Just see if they can sit and watch an interesting movie or video for at least an hour. If they can focus that long it is a usually a curable attention problem! It is a problem of <u>in</u>tention rather than <u>at</u>tention that can be corrected without medication if the child CAN focus when motivated enough(such as a movie).

*GIVE NO NEGATIVE INPUT!! Only positive attention is given for the good parts. Silence is golden, use it to your advantage. If the child is lying down or talking, direct him to his room so they can rest and get strong enough to try again later. NO privileges until the sitting is correctly completed. Let him take his time doing it wrong first. Time starts when he is in position not when he announces that you may begin timing now. Talking is not part of good sitting.

*Sitting is not punishment, it is a thoughtful gift of time for your child to think and get control of him/herself. There are a number of religions that use this position to facilitate inner peace. I think we all need more of that! Try sitting !

*Three times each day for the first 6 months your child needs to have this quiet time to think given to them. Sometimes it will be when they are flashing warning signs and need to think before processing feelings; more often just to practice getting control and getting stronger.

* Strong sitting should always end with a big hug and smiling eye contact

*REMEMBER: You must get compliance on this basic level before attempting to get compliance, honesty, or any progress on any level. The choice is (___) minutes of "strong sitting" or 2 hours of "wimpy sitting" if you are dancing with the resistance rather than hitting it head on. If you are hitting it head on, be sure and do it when you have two days to read and relax with one eye on your sitter. It might take them a long time to get it clear you are serious, and that you are willing to wait patiently until they get strong enough to do it right. "No problem!" I like to say. That means it's no problem for me! The child should have all units of concern.

Just say no! An explanation weakens your position of authority if you have to explain your decision. This is not a cue for the child to start whining . I like to have "NO! practice". I have the child ask me for any five things. To each request I say "No." with loving eye contact. When they are quiet and handle it, I grab them up, twirl them around, and say, "WOW! You are getting sooooo strong! I just said no and you didn't whine and fuss! Great job!!!"

For some children with a case of jabber mouth, I withdraw their talking privilege. All they are allowed to say 7 things: "Yes, Mom" or "Yes, Dad". Thank you, Good night, May I please have a drink?, May I please go to the bathroom?, May I please be excused from the table? When they have handled that for one full week correctly, I return their entire talking privilege. They usually have to start at the top again sometime within the first month. Each time they lose control of their mouth they are telling me they need an extra day of practice. I respect them letting me know they need lots of practice. They usually earn 10 to 20 extra days before they realize I'm serious.

The basic skills -come, go, no, sit, stay- should be mastered, according to Dr. Foster Cline, by 18 months of age. They MUST be mastered before a child can possibly handle more involved tasks, such as chores and school. Have fun practice sessions when you have some extra time. Use lots of smiles, pizazz, and hugs!

Choices are added after the child has begun to let go of control and clearly allow the adults to be in charge. Trusting the parents is first. When they have displayed a week or more of consistent trusting without testing, offer them a choice of two items. This might be milk or juice. If they pick a third choice, you know they are not ready for choices and wait a few weeks or so before trying again. Choices might be: Do you want to go to the park or the pool? Do you want to read or draw? Do you want a drumstick or a wing?, etc. You make the choices until they are ready. They have enough to decide in the beginning: to do it your way and win or choose to lose.

REMEMBER:
ACTION
NOT
ANGER!

CHAPTER FIVE: <u>SETTING LIMITS- HELPING YOUR CHILD TO ACCEPT LIMITS</u>

The richness of the human experience would lose something of rewarding joy if there were no limitations to overcome.
Helen Keller

A child feels safe when the loving parent is strong enough to be in control. When the parent sets limits and maintains established limits, the child can learn to trust. A CHILD WILL NOT LEARN TO TRUST SOMEONE WHO IS WEAKER. If he is "out of control," he believes you are not strong enough to control him or to keep him safe so he takes more control, becomes more hyper, learns slower, and regresses.

Setting Limits is the concept of being strong, being in control and being respected by your difficult child. It also creates a safe home environment for all your children. Clearly defined and maintained limits also work for the parents' well being. By being in control of your child's physical location and behavior, you minimize confrontations with them and have the ability to tend to your own needs. Sometimes you must meet resistance with resistance. Sometimes you need to learn to dance with the resistance. YOU MUST BE IN CONTROL.

The setting of limits includes the understanding that a violation of those limits results in consequences. Remember that the consequence must not be imposed in anger or out of your own frustration. Keep soft eye contact, keep calm and keep control.

When your child can live peacefully within the limits you set, you then can expand the limits. Children earn privileges by being able to live within the set limits. They are living within the set limits when they are no longer challenging them. Giving the child unearned privileges will cause regression and delay the healing process of bonding.

It's not the parent's job to make the child happy; it is the child's job to make the parents happy with the child. "If momma ain't happy, ain't nobody happy."

<u>In the beginning, your child should learn to ask for everything</u>. They must ask to go to the bathroom, to get a drink of water, EVERYTHING. When it starts to feel like they must ask to breathe, you are on the right track.

Knowledge is power, don't give it away by informing the child of plans and scheduled events, use a need-to-know basis. Do not inform him when you are planning fun events. He will sabotage them. Do not tell him when therapy is scheduled; he will put on a facade in order to fool you into a lighter session because he is "doing well". Do not share when visits are scheduled that may be difficult. It gives him time to worry himself into a frenzy. Also if the visit or event is then cancelled for some reason he could be disappointed and angry.

The alarm on the bedroom door establishes a very clear physical limit for the child. When the alarm is working , day or night, the child can be controlled by being placed in the bedroom. CONSEQUENCES: There needs to be a very substantial consequence for opening the door after being told not to. In my house, for children over 5, it is 100 to 500(depending on their age) pushups interspersed throughout the day for a number of days and no privileges until they are complete. Do not expect any child to do more than 30 jumping jacks or push-ups at a time! The child should not be put in their room for more than 30 minutes twice a day unless there is an emergency or the child is ill.

Stealing. Your child should not be permitted to "borrow" things (or obtain undeserved "gifts") from others. The excuse that a stolen item was "loaned" by a friend must be avoided. CONSEQUENCES: Any suspected stolen items are paid back double.

Teasing animals. CONSEQUENCES: The *first time* consequence is to lose all animal privileges for a minimum of three months. This includes talking to the animal, touching or petting, feeding, walking and initiating contact. The child must earn the privileges back or re-home the pet. You may choose.

Bedtime is not optional! Uncontrolled bedtime (room time) is a power drain. . Set it up clearly by 7:00 for younger children, or 8:00 for older children. No later! CONSEQUENCES: For every minute your child delays past going to his room, or every minute he makes annoying noise in there, assign an extra chore. No reminders by you. He goes to sleep whenever he chooses.

Misbehaving in public, especially shopping. Children think they can not be controlled in a pubic setting. Wrong! While grocery shopping, the one in control pushes the cart and your child has both hands on the side of the cart. If the child accepts this limitation - no whining or wiggling - for five or six shopping trips, they graduate to one hand on the cart. After they can handle one hand on the cart, they may walk quietly next to you. Next, permit the child to assist with the shopping, sending them for items and teaching them to shop. Explain selection, price comparison and practice counting. CONSEQUENCES: If the child will not stay within these limits, he goes back to the beginning - both hands on the cart or no shopping with parent until they are more emotionally stable. I do NOT recommend having children do push-ups, jumping jacks, or sitting in public. The opportunity for the child to attract and suck a passer-by into a pity party could destroy your efforts.

Whining or begging for things/grabbing or touching things while in a store. Ask, "Did you bring money? Is this your birthday?" Hands can stay in pockets or thumbs through belt loops or give them something to carry with both hands. Powerful parents do not regularly purchase gifts, certainly not weekly or monthly.

Meals. All meals are eaten together around the table with the TV and radio off. In the beginning, parents serve the food without asking the child's preferences. A disturbed child does not go throught the kitchen and eat their findings. Meals are an important part of nurturance. They must be prepared and dicided on by the adults. Give very small portions to picky eaters with second helpings always available when the plate is empty. At home and in restaurants, Mom decides what the child eats. Keep the child's least favorite foods to a minimum, but do serve them. CONSEQUENCES: If the child does not eat everything on the plate, they are obviously too full for dessert. Your child does not eat out until they eat properly at home. In a restaurant, you order for the child until they are completely under control (usually months) No "What do you want, sweetie?" (translates to "How may I serve you your highness?") You decide. You order. Only when mealtime limitations are accepted for at least one month may the child begin to make meal choices.

Telephone. Kids think you have no control when you are on the phone. When the phone rings or before you make a call, your child goes to their THINK WITHIN SPOT. (see Chapter Five) This rule stays in place until the child does it well for at least one month. Be kind, keep phone calls to 10-15 minutes.

Play time. In the beginning, play time is limited to reading, mini tramp, constructive activities like Legos®, Lincoln Logs® and coloring with washable crayons. Set clear limits at the beginning of the activity! Play time lasts until the child talks or moves out of the set boundaries, such as a corner of the room for construction or a chair for art/reading. One word or step out of set boundries by the child means play is over; the remaining time is spent doing strong sitting or working.

Wild haircuts and clothing. Gangster or drug-lord wanna be hair do's or clothing are not financed by parents or other educated adults. Period.

Privilege Schedule - Freedoms must be earned! They are earned by being respectful, responsible and fun to be around. Goal setting is an important skill. Help your child set goals for privileges he wants to have. Let him earn them in his own time. No pushing. No reminding. Keep the tight beginning-level structure until he is ready. Expect the child to take weeks or even months before they get motivated and begin to reach for new freedoms. If they take a long time earning things, be glad they are letting you know they are not ready for more. Do not feel frustrated. Be happy your child is handling what freedom they do have rather than complain!

Setting Up the Goals

When your child has been handling the beginning (Lego®) level by no longer testing the set limits, he will soon be ready to expand his boundaries. When he has been compliant long enough to become motivated to be interested in other things, he will ask to do more. This is the signal that it is time to set up his Privilege Schedule. Have him do strong sitting to think of privileges he is interested in earning. For a younger child, make a list as he tells you what he would like to be able to do. An older child should write his own list. After you have the list from the child, on your own or with your spouse, decide what skills the child should demonstrate before he gets each privilege and for how long. A rough guideline begins on the next page. You may add to or leave things off according to your lifestyle and availability of activities in your area. The time limits are the ones I use for most children. Set your own according to what your child is and is not handling.Tailor it to your liking. Write it down in a clear format and then review it with the child. Expect him to be angry that you are in charge and things he used to do are now special privileges to be earned. It's okay to be angry. Having him express the feelings in words is very important. Hug him and be understanding say, "I bet this is hard for you!". Remember to again give him an opportunity to share feelings and end with the list being posted in a good spot and a big hug! As other things come up, add them to the list.

Privilege Schedule

Privileges MUST be earned, or the child will act out or disobey set boundries to let you know they can't handle so much.

Examples of possible requirements are: being respectful, responsible, and fun to be around. An example of being respectful would be saying "yes, mom" or "yes, dad" with eye contact. An example of being responsible would be: caring for self, personal possessions , and doing chores fast and snappy and right the first time, making his bed daily, remembering to take medications with no reminder. Examples of being fun to be around would be: no unscheduled tantrums, being considerate to siblings, controlling their own stealing, lying, or destruction. I also try to tie in something pertaining to the goal such as not messing with the pets in order to earn their petting privilege. It is better to have a child earn and reach for privileges rather than lose them. They have a feeling of accomplishment ! See Page 95 for more ideas.

These goals are cumulative, only being taken away rarely and if absolutely necessary.

Children need to have play time everyday!

Fun activities that _do not_ require earning:
reading (book is selected by parent)
Legos®, Lincoln Logs®, toy farm sets, erector sets, etc.(for thinking, planning, problem solving, attention problems)
drawing/coloring (washable crayons only)
jumping on a _mini_ tramp (with adult present)

One day of doing set requirements, can earn _one_ of the following:

jumping rope(soft handles)

hopscotch (alone)

soft jacks

reading (parent gives choice of 2-3 books)

playing on swings/slide (with no other children present)

playing in sandbox with plastic toys (alone)

playing with clay or playdough

doing extra work to earn money

One week of consecutive success with requirements can earn one of the following:

collections, i.e.. baseball cards, pogs, match box cars, stamps, coins

family outings/pool, zoo - in town

eating out (a good requirement is correct table manners for one week)

One month of consecutive success with requirements can earn all of the following:

receiving phone calls ("I'm sorry ...can't come to the phone right now. May I take a message?" Do NOT embarrass child by explaining restrictions to callers)

going out to play - away from mom

answering the door

playing Nintendo or other expensive family toys

mountain climbing

sledding - in family yard

sitting in the front seat of car

selecting their own food, McDonald's or other restaurants

ordering magazines and cereal prizes

wearing a wrist watch

horseback riding

having a birthday party

Christmas gift exchange (should have earned money for gifts or hand made
      thoughtful gifts to give to all family members. NO handouts from parents!!)

going to movies - with family

shopping - with parent holding hand (No, teens do not hold parent's hand)

opening windows in car - without permission

Two months of consecutive success with requirements can earn one or more of the following:
making calls on phone (must have purpose, not just to chat)
pets-touching them (also must not sneak touching them for 2 months)
watching TV and/or Movies (one or two times per month maximum)
walkman
going to Sunday school - without parents
school field trips (must have earned and handled school and home for two months)

Three months of consecutive success with requirements can earn the achiever one or more of the following:
using computer
using vacuum and some power tools (NOT power saw /drill/chain saw)
attending school
radio and CD players
playing with other kids in the family with adult involved
having cash in their possession
shopping without holding parent's hand

Six months of consecutive success with requirements:
answering phone(must also be educated enough to write messages well)
have a friend over (not overnight)
go to friend's, neighbor's, Grandma's house
athletics (on a team)
Pets-controlling them(walking, giving commands, holding, touching, or sleeping with)
church activities/youth group - without parents
bicycles
joining band and/or choir
staying up late
skateboarding
rollerblading
skating
selecting clothing purchases
decorating room

riding school bus

tattling (telling to get help for someone rather than to get them in trouble)

getting out of room in the morning without having to be let out

playing with other kids in the family with adult near by

family outings - out of town

going to movies - without family

One year:

scouts/girl or boy, 4-H, FFA, pony club, etc.

pets-having their own (must work through levels from plant to pet)

pushing shopping cart

music lessons

skiing

snowboarding

BMX-motor bikes, dirt bikes

talking in car

playing with other kids in the family without an adult present

sleeping out in yard

camping - w/ family

purses, jewelry, wallets

no alarm (1-2 years)

having potential weapons in room (crayons, markers, safety pins,
        batteries, scissors, glue, rocks, or pens)

pocket knife (12 years old or above)

using power lawn mower (also 12 years old or above)

television

dating

Two years:

karate or self-defense training

cooking (or 17 years old or above)

driving a snowmobile, ATV, or 4-wheeler

driver's license (for some) Child never steers or drives without license.

motor cycles

gum - chewing

owning wanna-be gang or drug-lord clothing, hair-do's

Two-five years:
shooting a weapon (target practice)
having potential weapons in room (must be at least 12 years old) (lighters, matches, scissors, baseball bat, hockey stick, bows and arrows)

After graduation from high school:
Driver's license or permit (for most)
Having a job
owning a TV/VCR
own bb gun
pay for half of a car (child pays other half)
steering the car without a driver's license or permit

After graduation from college (or never)
giving unearned money (allowance)or loans without excellent collateral IN YOUR HANDS (privately funded welfare)
parents purchasing car
co-signing loan (for car or anything else)
own a rifle, handgun, hunting bow,or crossbow

GOAL WORKSHEET Example

PRIVILEGE TO EARN TIME	PARENT EXPECTATIONS	LENGTH OF
Earning Extra $	do regular chore fast, snappy, + right	One day
Play in sandbox alone	Be respectful, responsible+put toys up	One day
Go to McDonalds	Eat nice at home with good manners	One week
Have a wrist watch	be responsible for body, stuff, +chore	One month
Go to movie with us	Be respectful, responsible+ fun to be with	One Month
Using the computor	Have damage deposit earned +be responsible	3 months
Using vacuum	Have damage deposit earned +be responsible	3 months
Play with brother	Be respectful, responsible+fun to be with	4 months

♥   A critical piece in the puzzle of parenting is the correct balance between nurture and structure. The child will try to sabotage each piece. Some are better at sabotaging nurturing, while others are more skilled at breaking down structure. With too much structure and not enough nurturing, the child feels the mom is "too tough and too cold " and will not bond because they do not feel safe. They don't heal.

♥   With too much nurturing and not enough structure, the mom feels "mean" and so "cuts the child slack". This eliminates the needed structure. The child feels the mother is weak and does not trust and love because the consequences don't happen, unearned privileges are given and/or restitution is not required. The child is given too much; he doesn't feel safe, He doesn't heal.

♥   The amount of snuggle time and hugs must equalize the rules and expectations. In the beginning, there must be a tremendous amount of both. As the child heals, less are needed, until ideally, the hugs are seven a day and no structure is required because the child no longer needs it. He must develop his own conscience and self control rather than having to be controlled by others. Parenting out of guilt, pity or power tripping is not in balance. You'll know you found the balance when your child feels safe enough to grow emotionally, and become responsible and appreciative! You will be happier too!!

CHAPTER SIX: SUPERCHARGE YOUR EXPECTATIONS OF RESPONSIBILITY

People have a way of living up or down to your opinion of them.
                                                              Jane Wells 1886

A child will rise to the level of expectation. It is the parent's job to set that level of expectation. As with setting limits, this is a continuation on the themes of learning self control and respect for others and himself.

Be certain that each task given to your child is reasonable and one that can be accomplished.

IT IS THE CHILD'S RESPONSIBILITY TO...

CLEAN HIS OWN ROOM. The child makes his bed every morning before he is allowed out of his room. This starts the day with the child being responsible. If the child refuses, he spends half the day in the bed then is given another opportunity to be responsible about his bed. A Saturday ice cream party includes all those in the house with clean and vacuumed rooms.

SELECT HIS OWN CLOTHING. The child selects what he will wear each day and dress himself with no reminders, by a certain time. The child should have seven outfits, including socks and underwear, appropriate for the season to select from. Box up out of season or excess clothing. He does not come out of his room in the morning until he is dressed.

HELP WITH THE LAUNDRY. Each week, without being reminded (if he is 5 or over), the child should be expected to bring his laundry, including sheets and towel, to the washer on his designated laundry day. He then sorts the whites and darks. You must communicate the schedule to your child. After the laundry is washed and dried, by an adult or a nondestructive child 9 or older, the child should fold the clothing exactly mom's way. When finished, the child does good sitting next to his work, waiting for you to check it. This is an important opportunity to give positive attention. The clothing is then carried to the bedroom and put away.

TAKE CARE OF URINE OR FECES PROBLEMS. Angry children often urinate or defecate out their anger. This mess must be completely cleaned up by that child. He is expected to bring the soiled bedding, clothing, toys, rugs, etc., fill a bucket with cold water and one cup white vinegar, take the bucket outdoors and rinse the items. I fill and carry the bucket for the younger children. He then gives you the rinsed items to wash and dry, the child remakes the bed. It is his job to keep his room smelling good, carry extra clothing and plastic to sit on, until he is strong enough to talk out feelings rather than pee them out!

DO THEIR CHORES

Work is love made visible.
Kahlil Gibran

 Daily chores (equal to about 30 minutes of your effort) should be and must be expected for the child to heal. A minimum of 6 days a week, a chore to help the family must be completed before playtime and before meal time. Simply say, "Feel free to join us for dinner when your chore is finished." NO, cleaning his room and baking cookies do NOT count as family chores. Doing the same chore everyday helps the child become proficient in life skills and helps him learn how to give, helping the family. The parent selects the chores appropriate to the child's functioning level. Start with simple chores such as sweeping and let him practice daily until he can do them fast, snappy and right the first time for 7 consecutive days. He then graduates to a more advanced chore. Washing dishes is the most advanced chore. He should be proficient at bathroom cleaning, vacuuming, dusting, floor scrubbing, yard raking, etc., before being advanced to a chore that is done after dinner. Dishes not washed correctly or in a timely manner disrupts the entire family and can cause illness. Dinner dishes in our home are done by everyone. One washes, one rinses and dries, one wipes counters, one sweeps, one puts leftovers away and one washes the pots and pans. No one leaves the kitchen until it is all finished. This encourages a spirit of cooperation among the crew.

 What age do chores start? Between the ages of two and three, a child can sweep the porch, fold washcloths, fetch items, match socks, help set the table.

You teach him how to do each chore over a period of days by working side by side to complete the task. After you are sure your trainee is clear on your expectations, cut him loose to give it a spin. Yes, he will fail repeatedly until he figures it out. It's okay; don't blow up over left-over dirt on the floor. Just have him practice until he gets it, and remind him how lucky he is to have an awesome parent like you to be such a patient teacher!

When the task is completed the worker does "strong sitting" facing the chore until the parent comes and checks the job. Sitting is used to teach the child patience and self discipline. It also eliminates the hassle of the child announcing to the parent that the child is ready for the parent to check the job. The job should be checked when correct sitting, near the parent, has been long enough for the child to decide if the child really wants it presented the way it's been done. Usually a few minutes of strong, straight sitting is sufficient.

Thoroughly checking the job is important for several reasons: 1. It shows that you care about the child's effort. 2. It's important to be thorough when checking a chore. The child may try to pull a fast one by intentionally leaving part undone. The child may view the parent as dumb and the child as smarter if he is able to con or sneak by with inadequate work. 3. Checking the chore gives the parent an excellent opportunity to help build the child's self esteem by using some positive pizazz, loving eye contact, and, of course, a hug. When the adult takes the time to really check a job and finds it done well, the resulting praise (pizazz) is powerful. A child who sees himself as a good worker, even excellent at certain tasks is better equipped to handle life in the real world.

The job is done correctly when it is done the way you, yourself would have done it well. Teaching A+ floor scrubbing and laundry folding is how a child learns to do A+ science projects in school and A+ work in the job market later in life. You teach him how to put out the extra effort to finish a job he can be proud of, and he learns how to take pride in work and in himself. How a shirt is folded or the laundry is sorted seams unimportant, but it is the basis for every effort he will put out in life! Note: A positive way to handle errors in a chore would be to point to the well done areas and remark, "I really like this part, here. When you get this other part done just like this, it will be great!" These skills need to be learned at home while the child has loving parents to help support and encourage. As an adult, your child will need to complete tasks for an employer who will not be lenient.

Doing chores is a good barometer for therapy. If the child repeatedly does chores wrong, or "forgets" them, it indicates the child is internally out of control, angry, and rejecting bonding. This child needs professional help pronto! (See Page 21 for selecting a therapist)

Caring for younger children, plants, animals or cooking are NOT appropriate tasks. No power tools, vacuum etc., until the child is old enough and has been nondestructive for two to three months. Preparing meals is a way we nurture our families. Children who do not trust, and want to be totally self reliant, often use their cooking skills to push the family away. This makes him feel like he does not need anybody else. Cooking together on a special project, such as Christmas cookies, can be a very bonding experience shared with love. A child needs to be healthy and making good decisions for a period of several months, at least, before being taught to prepare meals other than a bowl of cereal or a sandwich. Asking a child with attachment problems to do pet or child care is a set up for failure. It is not recommended until a child has done well in all areas for several years. If you choose to have a child help you while you care for pets or children, it can be a good learning experience for the child. They can learn to mimic you as you model caring and gentleness toward others.

When he doesn't want to work, he needs to sit and rest until he gets over it. Soup kitchen meals are usually served and no privileges until he motivates himself to become part of the family by pitching in to do his part. Jobs completed correctly the first time are always rewarded with pizazz and sometimes, if it's extra work, pay or gifts. Usually half salary is paid for a job needing to be done twice. The third time a job is done over is always the last and he often needs a change of pace before resuming work. When a child has messed up a chore twice, it is obviously a red flag calling for help from the parent. Sometimes simply pulling the child up on your lap and processing feelings (see Chapter 11) before having the child attempt the task for the third time will release the tension enough to obtain compliance from the child. Occasionally more than talking is needed. Compliance in another area such as pushups, good sitting, or a very minor task helps break the roll down the drain on which the child has set his course. Asking a child to do 10 good push ups or 25 lousy ones sets it up to where the can't lose! Asking for 10 minutes of perfect straight-backed sitting or 30 minutes of lousy sitting is another way to both win! Jollying the kid out of a rut is another option. The tackle and tickle method can be a fun one if the parent knows when to stop on a loving note. Asking, "Who's my favorite laundry folder?" and tickling either until you get the answer ("Me") or until it is not fun for the child, can be a silly way to laugh them back on track. Sometimes his lack of effort is due to a severe ice cream deficiency. Push against shove does not work. If the parent is determined to force the child to do the job and the child is determined to not do the job, both lose. The goal is to build the child, not break the spirit.

Remember: The job is not as important as the child.

EARN THEIR OWN MONEY a problem child is not given an allowance (privately funded welfare). Do not pay the child for doing their chores or helping the family. To earn money for extra things and to pay for damages or restitution, the child may be paid for doing additional tasks. Pay minimum wage according to how long it would take you to do the job. If the job is not done correctly the first time, half pay. If the job is not done correctly the second time, no pay.

GET AN EDUCATION Your child must realize that going to school is a privilege. School is a "get to" not a "have to". It is not the parent's job to pound information into the child. The parent should not remind the child to do his homework. When your child comes home from school, he is to take his school bag up to his room, a room that is set up with a desk, chair, lamp, pencils, and paper. DO NOT ask about homework. As he eats his after-school-snack ask him what new things he learned today. What was the most fun he had? What was the hardest? Show an interest! Explain one time (in his life) that the time he spends in his room can be used wisely for homework if he chooses. Do not expect him to spend all day in a desk at school, walk in the door at home, and crack the books again. After the post-school snack and debriefing time, he should complete his chores and then play until dinner, help with dinner cleanup then read, draw or something quiet and relaxing till bath time. He should then be hugged and sent to his room early enough to have time to do homework or quiet activities of his choice. If the child does not want to go to school (or is suspended or expelled) the child must develop life skills that do not require reading, writing, or math. The child who stays home cleans the barn, washes windows, does housekeeping, car washing, all the "skills" that will make him employable without an education. Hopefully, they will be chores that will increase his motivation to treasure education.

Caring for a pet is NOT a job for a disturbed child. An out of control child should not ever own a pet. Having a pet is a privilege that must be earned. Start with letting the child have a house plant (spider plants are great). If the plant survives and thrives, with NO reminders from you, for three to six months the child can graduate to caring for a fish. Continued responsibility for three to six months , and a rodent, reptile, or bird can be earned. Only if the success continues for an additional three to six months does the child graduate to a larger animal. He must show adequate knowledge of care required and earn the money to purchase his own pet and equipment at each level. Burying a dead plant is a lot easier than a puppy! He should not be expected to feed or care for pets until he is healed!

BE RESPONSIBLE FOR SEXUAL ACTIVITIES It is your child's responsibility to ask for help with birth control. Trying to convince older children not to be sexually active by lecturing and threatening will not work. Keep open communication and teach responsibility. Children who do not receive enough touch at home will seek it elsewhere. Keep the loving hugs, back rubs and pats on the back at full volume during the teen years! Children who have been sexually abused will often continue the sexual behavior done to them on other children or themselves. You must eliminate the opportunity by using the alarm, prohibiting sleep overs and summer camp, and by never leaving another child who may be victimized unattended, not even for a few seconds!

One mom left her two RAD children in the car in front of the post office. She, of course, turned the car off and took her keys. She ran in to drop letters in the box and returned to find them in the back seat having sex in broad daylight in a public parking lot!

CHAPTER SEVEN: EXPECT RESTITUTION FOR DAMAGES

You will find men who want to be carried on the shoulders of others,
who think that the world owes them a living. They don't
seem to see that we must all lift together and pull together.
Henry Ford II

Your child is responsible for any and all damages which he caused. "Responsible" means that the value of the stolen or damaged property must be paid back at DOUBLE the value.

The child must earn money to pay for the damages they incurred. If the parent gives the child the money, the child learns nothing. If it is pulled from a savings account, they never miss it. They don't learn.

Parents sometimes make excuses for their child who steals because they are embarrassed to have a child who is a thief. Do not buy into your child's or your own excuses. Stealing is not "borrowing" or "just using". Stealing is stealing. Denial and "kept secrets" feeds the pathology of the child and makes them sicker.

If the child has a history of stealing and has had the opportunity to steal, treat any suspected incident of theft as if they are guilty. It does not matter if the child admits it or not. If you think the child might have stolen or broken something, go with your intuition. IT IS BETTER TO ERR BY BEING TOO TOUGH.

Full restitution or a designated daily portion of it, if it is a large sum, must be earned before the child has any privileges.

EXAMPLE: a dialog with a child when you suspect he stole the missing item:
Mom: I noticed the pillow on the couch is missing
Kid: I didn't do it!
Mom: Who has a problem with stealing?
Kid: I do, but I didn't do it this time , REALLY!!! (guilty whine)
Mom: What do you think I think?!
Kid: You think I did it!
Mom: Right! So you will replace it, and if I find out later that you really didn't do it, I will gladly pay you back! Got it?
Kid: Got it!

Interactions should always end with warm eye contact (smile) and a hug!

A child with a history of stealing and/or destruction should establish a damage deposit. This is money that the child has earned that is put aside for future need. The amount set aside is twice the amount of the most expensive cost so far incurred ($50 to $300). If the child doesn't steal or damage for minimum of one month the money can be returned to them at $5 per week. Remember, he must do his regular family chore fast, snappy and right the first time before he may have an opportunity to earn money (see: earn their own money, page 60).

Restitution is not only monetary. The child must repair or "make better" damages and injuries even though there is no absolute value. A fundamental repair is the APOLOGY. All apologies must be sincere and include eye contact. EXAMPLE: "I'm sorry for _____. I need to pay you back. Would you like me to _____ or _____? The advanced child is capable of deciding what the non-monetary restitution should be. This compensation should always be in the form of the child's time, that is, time that would have otherwise been spent as the child wished. In the beginning, you decide the compensation. Restitution is always more than the injury caused,

Hassling, when your child intentionally annoys or irritates you or someone else, requires the child to give back your time wasted in dealing with the behavior. The child gives with his time. Foot or back rubs are good restitution. If the child hassles a sibling, good amends would include doing the other child's chores for a number of days or vacuuming the sibling's room, folding this laundry, etc.

Legal problems will become larger and larger each time unless charges are pressed the first time by a caring parent or adult. Don't wait until the parent has been beaten up several times to call the police! Not pressing charges just protects the child from the consequences they need. One father even had his ribs broken by his nine year old angry son, his wife was battered, and no help was called until the child beat his sister bloody! Stop it the first time there is an assault, arson, or any other violent behavior. You cannot be a great parent from a hospital bed.

School consequences such as expulsion should be supported by the parents as the school is setting clear limits on behavior they will not tolerate. Do not take it personally. You are not the one they are expelling. It is intended to help, not hurt your child. Firm limits on all sides speeds up the healing process. Thank them!

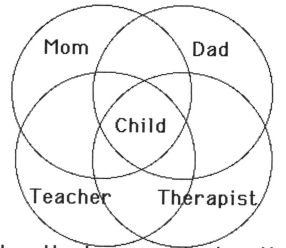

When the team works together
the child can feel safe enough
to trust and to begin healing.

CHAPTER EIGHT: REMOVE BARRIERS BETWEEN YOU AND YOUR CHILD

My mother loved children—she would have given anything if I had been one.
— Groucho Marx

Parents allow material objects to create a barrier between their child and themselves. It is essential to remember that your priority is your child and your relationship with him/her. The child's misbehavior should be considered a learning opportunity, not a personal attack. Your becoming angry at your child when her/his emotional condition causes an incident is like blowing up at the child for getting blood on the sheets after surgery.

Attempting to buy your child's love with material objects and privileges will not work. You cannot buy your child's good behavior, or bonding or healing. Excessive materialism takes the focus off love and the relationship and puts the emphasis on material things. Spending money on the child reinforces the child's negative behavior and impedes healing. Stop spending money, and spend time instead. It is a much wiser investment.

Removing barriers between you and your child

TELEVISION, VIDEO GAMES, RADIOS, WALKMAN - these are used to tune out relationships, feeling and thoughts. Turn them off and get rid of them. These distractions should be eliminated until the child is completely healed and the relationship with the parents is solid. Put them in the locked area.

In non-genetic ADD and ADHD, the damage done to the brain during the "age of Industry"(ages 2-4), when a child is learning to focus and problem solve, can be immense. During this age passive activity such as TV, video games, must be limited to one to two hours per week. Once that window of development in the brain is passed, in order for the child to be able to focus in school, and later in the job market, it is important to give the brain an opportunity to develop other channels to process information. It is ESSENTIAL that there be NO TV for six months to a year for healing to occur and that daily quiet time be spent building and problem solving with hands on materials such as Legos®, Constructs®, Lincoln Logs®, etc. I have had numerous successes with children graduating from special education into the regular classroom by giving their brains this healing time. They are easier to teach when their brain is working!

FURNITURE AND HOUSEHOLD OBJECTS - disturbed children often like to wreck things. If you have expensive furniture and other objects to which you are attached, remove these items and replace them with second hand things of less value, especially in the child's room.

TOILET PAPER , SHAMPOO, TOOTH PASTE, CLEANING SUPPLIES AND OTHER DISPOSABLE PRODUCTS - are often wasted by the child. This is a message that the child is volunteering to purchase that item for the family. This is behavior not to get angry about, just to deal with.

YOUR CHILD'S FRIENDS - can become a barrier if you are not prepared. This will be especially true if the child has privileges they have not earned, such as going to the movies or talking on the phone. A child will often find it easier to talk to peers rather than parents. On family outings such as church or movies, your child does not separate from your family to be with friends. The friend can join you under your supervision.

MEALTIME AND RUDE EATING HABITS - can become a barrier. It is important to calmly excuse the offending child to an outside picnic table or the laundry room and continue the meal in peace.

MUSIC LESSONS - should be provided only if the child asks. You pay for the first lesson and each lesson that follows a week of reasonable practice. Reasonable practice is determined by the instructor. If the child does not do the practice, the child pays for that lesson. Keep practice sessions from being a barrier.

DENTAL (ORTHODONTIC) BRACES - are not put on a child's teeth unless he has asked for them and has brushed two times a day for at least six months. If the child is not invested in the success of the braces, he will not wear the retainer and the teeth will move back. Even worse he will not brush his teeth while having braces and the massive decay will cause tooth removal.

CHAPTER NINE: AVOID THE WRONG BATTLES & WIN THE WAR AGAINST RAGE

*All men who have turned out worth anything have had
the chief hand in their own education*
                                        Sir Walter Scott

Choose battles you can win and choose them carefully . Do not get sucked into those battles that you cannot win. When you lose, you all lose.

The only time you get involved in a <u>battle between two children</u> is when your problem child is much stronger than a sibling or friend. Even then, you are the director between friends and siblings, NOT the referee or the detective. Arguing children, if equally matched, should be sent outside for a minimum 30 minutes to work out their differences. After 30 minutes, open the door and check for smiling faces. Ask if the issue has been resolved, no details, please. If both kids are not smiling, close the door for another 30 minutes. When both kids are happy, let them know what a proud parent you are because they learned diplomatic relations.

Give your child all the <u>UNITS OF THE CONCERN</u>. These units are how much each of you cares about the subject. If you care more than the child, NO changes will be made. You must let go and let them learn by their mistakes. Regardless of the responsibility - homework, hygiene, - the child is responsible for ALL of them. Quit worrying, feeling ashamed and embarrased! Let the child worry, feel ashamed, and embarrased for his own behaviors!

<u>Tell the child what to do rather than what not to do.</u>
EXAMPLES - 1. Sit on your hand rather than stop playing in your food. Give me the straw rather than stop blowing bubbles in your milk. A wise parent then withholds the straw the next few times with no comment.

<u>Prevent disasters</u>- No catsup, sauce, pop or milk in car. Drive through restaurants serve water. It is much easier for a child to clean up. Do not take the child out in public when he can't control himself at home! Have him earn it!

Food issues are impossible to control. You cannot make them swallow! Your child will put into his mouth what he wants to put into his mouth and the more you try to control it the more weird choices he will make. This has escalated from green beans to eating toothpaste and rocks as the child shows the parent he will control his own mouth. Sickening snack choices such as used gum from a sidewalk, boogers, or worms can be dealt with in fun ways.

Option: Upon seeing this gross intake by your favorite gourmet, you may reply, "Oh, good! I love it when kids find their own lunch/dinner. I was going out to Mc Donald's. This will save me money now that you've already eaten."

Option: for a child seen selecting tasty sidewalk snacks. "I'm so glad you don't mind touching gross stuff. Before lunch, I want you to collect ten pieces of used gum and put it in a nice line for me to see. This is a great way to help clean up our environment. Good thing we have you!"

Amount of food is not a good control battle. Sometimes, a child is sincerely not hungry. The old adage of eating everything on your plate has set up over-eating problems in many adults. Forcing your child to eat food he hates is always a lose-lose situation.

Option: A child facing a serving of broccoli can be laughed out of it by telling him he's not old enough to eat it. He still has child's taste buds. As his tastes mature, he will learn to like it. "For now, I get yours!"

Option: "You don't like the dinner? No problem! Our dog loves my cooking! You're excused. "This quickly teaches appreciation!

Option: When a child asks what he gets to eat because he doesn't want what you have prepared for dinner, a fun reply is, "Breakfast."

Food hassles can lead to drug abuse. A child forced to be vegetarian or on a sugar- free diet or any case where certain foods are withheld, often, as soon as they are able, will put in their body exactly what they want. Commonly, it's drugs. Teaching your child how to take care of himself by example and giving lots of permission for the child to make wise decisions is the best way to teach your child how to eat. If you choose to eliminate certain foods from your diet, that is your freedom. Forcing your food opinions on your child will cause problems.

Option: Give your child the information needed to make his own decision. Share with him your beliefs, purchase good food and only keep food you approve of in your home. You cannot control what your child puts in his mouth in your absence. If you try to do so, you will fail and your child will pay for your failure. Often teenagers need to rebel with food for several years but if taught well, with love, will return to your wise instruction. Parents with these issues need to relax.

Caution: A child with a health condition requiring a special diet can be driven to drug abuse by an overzealous parent!

<u>Friends</u> that your child chooses are a direct reflection of your child's self image. Parents get so concerned the child will learn bad things from peers that they freak out. The odds are, your child will rub off on them. You have no control over who your child chooses to spend time with in school. Because a child needs to feel accepted by his peers, it is very painful when a parent tears his selection to shreds verbally. When you tear down his friends you tear down your child.

    <u>Option</u>: "I would like to see your friends because I know kids pick friends that are as healthy as they are. I would like to meet your friends, so I can see how well you're doing. If you're hanging out with the kids that get into trouble lots, when can you bring a friend home for me to meet?"

    <u>Option</u>: "Your choice of friends is interesting. As you get healthier, I'll be curious to see who you'll pick for friends."

<u>A hair do</u> is a statement of "who your child is". If you want your child choosing a very rebellious hairdo, simply demand your choice of hair style repeatedly as the child grows. As soon as the child has the means to select his own hairdo, he will. If your son shows up with two foot tall purple spikes, or your daughter has her head shaved, you are not required to look at them. They still need your love. A nice solution would be to assure them in order to dine with you, they will wear a hat.

    Children who are making bad decisions, being rude, and acting inappropriately, often lose their hair spray, moose, or gel, privilege. Often, bizarre hairdos require these products and will go limp and look better without them. Warning: this often causes the child to keep a supply on hand at a friend's or in the school locker. You have no control over these places. Don't even try! You will lose. You can win in your home while your child is with you. Fun family activities often require a child to be clean with appropriate appearance. The child then may stay home or go to day care. Caution: Do not leave the child feeling rejected and unloved. It is very, very important to let him know he is very loved and that you are taking care of yourself by not choosing to be humiliated in front of family and friends.

Option: Take him to church on Sunday, a ball game, sports activity, or a swimming pool with the hairdo and act as if nothing is askew. Let the stares and the snickers from others get the message through to the child. Often this technique works much more rapidly than anything you could say.

Combing your child's hair until he is in first or second grade does not give him the practice that he needs to develop the skills to care for himself. Four year olds should be starting to comb their hair every morning.

Personal Hygene - Children with low self esteem often have trouble bathing, shampooing, teethbrushing, changing under garments and selecting clean clothes. Smelling good is not a prerequisite for love. We are capable of loving all kinds of smelly creatures. The best approach is to give the child the responsibility and stand back. It must be the child that carries all the concern over these issues. Give much more attention for doing it right than for doing it wrong!

Bathing/showering is a difficult issue. Getting your child to bathe can be easier if the child has to ask to take a bath. If you order him to bathe he will often just waste time and materials. A disturbed child may choose to push people away with his body odor. It's hard to hug a child and hold your breath, but it can be done!

Option: Weather permitting, plan a dinner at a restaurant but pack a sandwich for the offending child (PB & J). The child remains outside and eats the sandwich.

Option: In order to eat at the dinner table, each child is expected to get cleaned up for dinner. This means hair is combed, hands are washed, child smells OK. If this criteria is not met, the child eats his meal in the laundry room.

Option: A smell-good chart, strategically placed on the wall across from the toilet, sometimes helps. Star stickers are placed on the chart, by the child, each day he chooses to wash himself. This way, the child is taking all the units of concern. It is there, as a reminder, every time the child sits on the pot. This method builds self esteem in the child as he rewards himself with stars or smiley faces.

Option: Have your child (10 or younger) join you daily and brush your teeth, comb your hair, wash your face, together. Setting an example is the best way to start good habits for your child. As he internalizes your toothbrushing method, it's fun to observe the tiny details he picks up and copies from your daily ritual.

Note: When the stench of maggots encircles your child to the degree he is no longer huggable, beware. If your child gets too smelly (three months without a bath is the record at my house), and is pushing this hard to keep you at arms length, intensive therapy is required!

Option: Have the child put on swimming trunks if needed and bathe him yourself just as you would a younger child. This must be done lovingly. Try singing "rubber ducky" while you scrub! It is important to give a clear message that you will love this child and do anything necessary in order to continue to hug, hold, and be close to the child. Done lovingly, you can both win on this one.

Option: A child old enough to walk home *safely* may be let out of the car the last half mile or so to give the family noses a rest.

Option: You can try having a Saturday night "Salon Night" where you focus on fun. Wash the child's hair in the sink and try new hairdos. Be sure there is lots of laughing, eye contact and fun for both of you.

Tooth brushing is a health issue as well as a social issue when your child's grin is green. Pizazzing the positive is much more effective on toothbrushing than any other technique.

Option: Pay for the yearly cleaning and checkups and have your child pay for any cavities or extra cleaning required.

Option: Have your child pay for weekly cleanings at the dentist. Caution: Giving gifts of toothbrushes, toothpaste, combs, soap, brushes, is not effective and often backfires. The child must carry all the units of concern on personal hygene issues. These are not taken as loving gifts. They are usually received as inuendoes that you care more about his teeth than he does. Consider how you personally would feel unwrappping a gift of deodorant or mouth wash. When he does ask for a toothbrush, toothpaste, let him select a fun one to help motivate him to use it.
Caution: Children have been known to become drunk on certain mouthwashes.

Makeup - Many of the young girls with RAD try to hide the ugliness they feel inside by loading on the make up. If it is to cover acne scarring get them help. When you feel the time is right, this issue can be kind of a fun one. Shopping with your seventh or eighth grade student to purchase makeup can be a bonding experience. The mom and daughter, going in to have a facial and professional make over, can have a special time together. There are companies that will send a representative right to your home! We like to have some mother/daughter friends over and get more feedback on the outcome! In order to ascertain the appropriate age in your community for the child to begin wearing makeup, check it out. Go to the school, spend time with students, and see for yourself. If most of the sixth grade girls are wearing makeup and your child is forbidden, you will be setting up potential damage for your child's self image. And the reverse is also true if your child is the only one, or one of the very few, to be wearing makeup. It is not wise.

Option: If your daughter wants to begin adding color to her face before her time, you may share with her that younger children have a pure, natural beauty that fades with age: that she will need makeup to help cover the loss of her natural beauty at some point; that you are glad she is not as ugly as some other girls that need to start wearing makeup earlier; that you are glad her cheeks are still rosy, her lips have nice color and her eyes still sparkle. Ask her to let you know when she finds her natural beauty fading, and you will help get her started.

Option: Share with your daughter the thought that girls who apply heavy makeup, lots of black around the eyes and neon lips are advertising that their bodies are available for sexual use (whores). The boys always know this and that it is, of course, very sad but true. Ask if she knows anyone who wears too much makeup and then listen, empathetically.

School work is 100% the child's responsibility. Do not interfere in any way with the child's studies. Do not check homework or even ask if he has homework. If the child asks for help with homework, then, if you feel the child needs it, help. Report cards belong to the child. It is his record of progress. It is not yours. Some parents feel the grades reflect on them as parents. Did they get an A as a mom or an F as a dad? The teachers in public and private schools do not grade the parents on the child's report card. Do not pay your child for grades. Do not punish your child for grades. Schools have their own built-in consequences for problems. Let the consequences fall. Each grade is available each year as many times as the child requires it. Pushing a child to pass a grade the child is not mature enough to handle, is wrong.

The Home School, concept is wonderful for regular children when the parent is qualified and dedicated. It is NOT an effective option for RAD children. It sets up major control battles between parent and child. The child not only loses his relationship with his mother over it, he loses the opportunity for an education. They often do not accept learning from mother figures well until they are well healed. If, for any reason, the child cannot go to school, I recommend hiring a tutor.

Bed wetting, pants soiling, the more you try to stop these issues, the more the child will escalate them. Many RAD children pee out their anger! One therapist described it as "pissed off!" You cannot stop the child from urinating on things or wetting their bed - not by intimidation, coercion, or bribes. A seven year old even had bladder surgery as one parent attempted to stop the bed wetting. No, it did not stop the problem. Never humiliate your child! Let him worry about it! Let go!!!

  Option: The child's room is expected to smell good. It is the child's responsibility to keep it that way. A bucket water, and vinegar should be available for the sheet rinser each morning. The issue is the odor of the room and not the cause.

  Option: Carry a plastic trash sack and newspaper in your car for pants wetters to protect your upholstery. The adults do not bring a change of clothing for the wetter over five years old. The wetter may choose to carry a spare. The child needs to take responsibility for his problem.

  Option: Tell the child to "Continue to 'urinate or deficate out his anger' until he is strong enough 'to talk it out' like a regular kid. No problem! Some kids get it faster than others. It will be interesting to see how long it takes you! "

Picking scabs, nose picking, thumb sucking, nail biting, knuckle popping, and public masturbating are all issues you cannot stop by nagging, reminding, threatening, or bribery. It hasn't worked so far, has it?! Often, telling the child to go ahead will make them stop. This often works well for other problems as well; it's called prescribing the problem.

  Option: give the child 15 to 20 minutes daily alone in his room or the bathroom for several weeks to do his "hobby." If you forget- have him remind you by doing the behavior.

Option: When you see the child masturbating (or whatever), say, "Oh! I see you need to spend time with your hobby. I want you to wash your hands, then spend --- minutes in the bathroom doing your hobby. Be sure to wash your hands when you're done. I want to see those clean hands when you come out." No big deal. It helps to call it something weird like scab collecting, booger collection, nasal excavation, etc .

Noise Issues - A child that is sent to his room for a while to give the parents a break occasionally will attempt to hassle the parents by making noise. If the parent is in a tolerant mood, it is best to totally ignore the behavior. If the child is doing it to annoy the parents but does not succeed, the behavior will be eliminated without energy output on the parents' part. When pounding, loud singing, crazy talking, etc. becomes annoying, there are several fun ways to handle the situation. Each option is handled in the spirit of fun without anger.

Option: One is to have the child be noisy in his room on your terms. "I want to hear loud fussing (singing, pounding - parent's choice) for one hour (or 30 minutes) before you may come out. I want you to get it out of your system in there where you are safe and not hassling the rest of us." This only works if the adult is prepared to actually have the child be loud at that time. A tired, over-stressed parent seldom is ready for this racket.

Option: If the child is "over heating " in his room, a trip outside to "cool off" may be the ticket. Two to three minutes of good sitting on a cold porch does wonders for a noisy child. Cool weather may require 5 minutes of good sitting. (I'm not talking below freezing, here!) Warm weather porch sitting does not usually work.

Option: Say, "You may have 30 minutes of quiet time in your room or two hours of noise making." Or you can change this to, "You may do ten minutes of good sitting or one hour of yucky sitting."

Option: Ask, "Do you think it is hassling me to have all that noise, now? Do you really want to do that? If it is that important to you, I'll be sure to make a good list of hassle time chores for you to do for me to pay me back."

Option: Throw yourself on the floor imitating the child's noises on an extremely exaggerated level: eyes rolling, feet flailing, arms wildly waiving - let it rip. Hug the child afterward, give no explanations and leave the room. (It's usually a good idea to warn your spouse, beforehand.)

Option: "Is that you making that noise? I thought a gorilla, martian, or crazy person might have escaped and been in here terrorizing you?! I'm glad you're all right! Do you think you'll be able to get it together soon so you can come out? I could sure use a good helper."

ALCOHOL and DRUGS and SEX present unique problems because you cannot heal a relationship with someone who is dead, whose brain is fried or who is dying of AIDS. Children will try alcohol. The wise parent needs to have a pact with the child that if the child ever has more than one drink, the child will call home and the parent will come and give them a ride. No question, no lectures, no hassling. If drinking becomes a repeated occurrence or if you suspect or have confirmed drug use (home tests are available), remove the child from the environment immediately. Get professional help at the first indications. Sex issues are hot items. When your daughter begins to act like a B-in-H (bitch in heat) or your son's penis exercises begin to be a community affair, your panic/hysteria will heighten the activity. Relax, remember when you were a teen?! To push your daughter into penis collecting simply forbid her to have sex. To push your son into more community affairs, ground him, especially from his favorite females. The normal urgings caused by the hormones that have been deranged by early sexual abuse cannot be stopped by the parents. Your child must carry 100% of the units of concern. Chastity belts are no longer available. To curb her whore-ableness or his stud-liness, build their self esteem early. The higher their self image is the less they will be to do self destructive behaviors. It is the parents' responsibility to communicate (before the age of 9) with the child about sex and sexually contracted disease. As your child enters puberty, increase healthy touch and hugging. Having your child earn his freedom helps him to become more responsible before he is out having to make tough choices.

Option: Once he has earned the right to date, let your child make the decision. You really cannot stop him, can you? This option is extremely difficult and yet one of the most effective. The covert message needs to be given clearly that you trust your child to do what is best for him. Make birth control available without hassles.

<u>Sex and younger children</u> - Climbing on Mom's or Dad's lap and inappropriately snuggling into the crotch or handling a breast are some of the ways children drop hints they need help! Youngsters acting sexually need to be told that the behavior is not acceptable and they obviously need to practice sitting on laps appropriately more often. Sexual behavior toward a parent is so offensive to many parents it is handled with total rejection by shoving the child off the lap rather than correcting the behavior. "Don't throw the baby out with the bath water." DO be cautious! A child displaying sexual acting out is waving a red flag for help! He should NOT be left alone with another child or animal until he is healed. Yes! He can molest or rape your cat or dog ! Unfortunately it is not uncommon with RAD children.

Option: Ask the child what he was feeling when he did the behavior. Allow him to express his sexual desire or curiosity verbally. Listen with understanding and compassion. This is the time to take advantage of a great opportunity to open communication about any sexual feelings your child has. If you meet his desires and questions aghast with horror, he will not feel safe to share again. Being understanding and compassionate *the first time* opens up vital communication that will be important years down the road. Remember if he can verbalize it he doesn't have to act it out!

CHAPTER TEN: <u>TEACH YOUR CHILD TO THINK FOR HIMSELF</u>

A mother is not a person to lean on but a person to make leaning unnecessary.   Dorothy Canfield Fisher

Your child must learn to think and make choices without being told, ordered, or otherwise commanded. Learning to think is the natural consequence of having to think. If a child experiences the natural consequences of his actions, that child will develop his own inner voice and innate learning ability. Natural consequences are life's learning opportunities and are much more effective than words. They get the brain going.

If the process of learning through natural consequences is interrupted, the child will have an inability to think for himself. This child is set up to listen for voices outside their head for direction and will be vulnerable to peer pressure and drug and alcohol abuse.

When the parent interrupts the process with reminders such as "Put your coat on", "Do you have your homework?", or "It's time to go to bed", the powerful, underlying message the child hears more clearly than the words is, "You are too stupid to think for yourself and solve your own problems. You need someone (like me) telling you what to do." When the parent does not let the child learn the obvious through natural consequences, the child is being set up to think that someone else needs to do his thinking.

<u>A child who demands action</u> by saying 'I'm hungry (thirsty, tired, hot, cold, etc.), is not communicating but insisting that the parent should solve the child's problem. This is complaining or griping. A powerful parent does not reinforce griping. Learn to politely thank your child for sharing this "information" with you. Acceptable dialogue includes your child politely asking, such as "May I please have a drink of water." Parenting is about teaching your child life skills. In the work place an employee does not stand with a broken pencil complaining to the boss that, "My pencil's broken."

<u>Do not lecture or nag</u> your kid. Let him think. Some parents yell so loud or talk so much that the child cannot hear his inner voice. Two sentences is usually the maximum that he hears before he tunes you out. Talk less!

EXAMPLES - Natural consequences.

If the child goes outside when it is cold without a coat, the natural consequence is that the child gets cold. If this happens often enough, the child will think to remember the coat.

If the child repeatedly stays up late, he will have to deal with being tired at school the next day. If homework isn't done, the natural consequences is the child dealing with the teacher. Hopefully it will be a teacher who will consequence swiftly with a zero grade for the paper and not a second chance.

It is the child's responsibility to make their play time interesting. A child who has not learned to think for himself assumes his parent is responsible for providing constant entertainment, like a cruise director. In the beginning, the child has few options for play time - reading, drawing and Legos®. When the child says "I'm bored", promptly give the child something else to do by having a chore ready. Scrubbing a floor is handy.

If your child runs away, you cannot make him stay. Shackles are illegal and it is impossible to work with a child who is absent. If the child has a history of running away, prepare for the next event by having a trained home ready for your child's placement. Do not tell the child you have made this preparation. When your child runs, call the police, then order pizza. Your life should continue. Let the police find the child. It is important the family does not pick up units of concern and spend energy trying to bring back a child who doesn't want to be there. When the police find the child, have the child taken to the prearranged, trained home for a few days/weeks. When the child returns home, it must be only by mutual agreement.

Telling your child what they should or should not do does not help them learn to use their brain. Certain privileges (all privileges must be earned) can raise special problems. If you tell your child he cannot see a particular movie because there is too much sex or violence, this is a strong message to the child that the child is weak and easily influenced. Instead of arguing or lecturing the child about why the movie is bad, simply refuse to finance or provide transportation. If the child uses his brain and finds a creative way to earn money and get transportation, going to the movie has done more good than the movie's content can do harm (I'm not encouraging or approving of children watching violent or sexual movies).

A disturbed child is not in touch with himself. He will stand with snot dripping down his face. It is permissible to wipe the nose of a two year old, but do not remind an older child. A child old enough to know better should be excused to his room without explanation, a simple "Sweetheart, you are not fun to be with right now. I want you to go to your room" will suffice. Let him have 15 to 20 minutes in his room to think. Then go and ask, "Why did I send you to your room?" When he has the answer and solution, he is congratulated, hugged and released.

The THINK WITHIN PLACE is included in this outline under Chapter V, Teaching Self Control, but is also an important tool in teaching your child to think. The purpose of the Think Within Place is not to punish but rather to give the child time to regroup. It is the gift of time. It should be used even when your child is having a good day. The concept is comparable to giving yourself, an adult, time to quietly sit each morning without distraction and organize the thoughts for the day. Another image is if, in the middle of a busy work day, your boss came to you and told you to take the next 20 minutes and do nothing but sit quietly and be with yourself.

The THINK WITHIN PLACE is a permanent spot in the home that is easily accessible. When sitting in the Place, the child is facing the wall (not covered in wall paper). The child sits with knees touching the wall and back straight. The mouth is closed and feet, fingers, and face are still. If there is a wetting problem, have the child sit on a washable rubber backed throw rug. It is important that the place be comfortable. By sitting straight, the blood and oxygen can freely circulate, and the child is not distracted. When the chest is open, the heart and lungs can work much more freely .

TIME IN is also a quiet time, but it is between your child and you. If your child is having a hard time being compliant or quiet he may need TIME IN. The parent sits in a comfortable chair - you can be reading. The child sits on the floor next to the chair with his forehead touching your leg (thigh) and his back straight. Gently and quietly stroke the child's back. No words or lecture - just quiet, calm, rubbing massage. The child can sit and make faces at your leg and work through his frustration. It is difficult for the child to maintain his anger while he is being loved in this manner.

Action increases thinking. Jumping jacks and pushups increase circulation, release body tension and improve brain clarity - Double the child's age is a good goal to work toward, starting with five excellent ones done to your high (but attainable) standards. This technique is used when the child's brain is stuck (symptoms of a stuck brain: he gives you hate looks like you did it; he stares rather than answer, or he says 'I don't know').

Another situation where action increases thinking is undoing damage he has done. The white socks worn in the yard with no shoes scenario. The child is volunteering to sit outside with a bucket of hot soapy water and a bar of laundry soap (no bleach), and scrub until the bottoms are as white as the top. "No rush, take your time." No privileges or other activities until it's done right. The child who cuts up clothing or rips buttons off can learn sewing and patching skills by practicing on scrap material before repairing his clothing. Supervise needle use. Children who won't wipe are asking to scrub unders.

Do not attempt to use punishment with RAD children. "Punishment" is used to cause "suffering for one's sins". It teaches revenge. "You did this. Now you must pay with pain and suffering." It is NOT helpful for children that have been abused. They often act like they are "itchin' for a lickin' " in order to get you to hurt them so they can fit you into a catagory with other adults they understand. Spanking, rageful yelling to intimidate, grounding to "make a child miserable so he will regret his foul deeds", are all tools that cause the child to be angry at the parent as the judge and sentencer. "Consequences" are used to teach the child to think about what he has done. It is not about suffering or being miserable to pay for bad behavior. It can even feel good. The consequence of buying flowers for someone is a happy smile. The consequence of kicking my dog is teeth holes in your leg. The consequence of wrecking your car is either expensive or walking a lot. The consequence for wearing white socks in the dirt is scrubbing them clean . Make a list of several dozen specific and general consequenses so you are ready. You know the behaviors your child does to push you away. Be ready next time!

Let him answer his own questions such as "What is for dinner? Where are we going? " A good response is: "How else can you find the answer to that question besides asking? " Let him think of the answer and then congratulate.

CHAPTER ELEVEN: GUIDE THE PROCESSING OF FEELINGS

*The work will wait while you show the child the rainbow, but
the rainbow won't wait while you do the work.*
                                        Patricia Clafford

A disturbed child may have internalized infantile rage and not internalized (taken in and made a part of himself) a powerful, loving parent. He often identifies with evil and destruction and is drawn to fire and gore. The parent and trained therapist must help the child process these feelings through a three part process: locate, validate and accept. "What are you feeling? I bet you do feel --- I can understand you feeling that way."

The child's unresolved anger or conflict will become evident in an event, often intentional destruction or violence. These events are the child asking for your help. It is very important to process feelings as quickly as possible after an event. When working with the child to develop an awareness of feelings, the initial simplified choices are: mad, sad, glad or scared.

Almost daily, ask your child, "on a scale of one to ten, how mad are you right now?" "one" being a tiny bit mad and "ten" being mad enough to kill. Be prepared to handle the child admitting to a "ten". There should be no shock, no surprise, or tension in your eyes. You need to be powerful enough to handle the full range of your child's feelings. If his depth of anger is to a killing rage, how large will his capacity for love and joy be?! I have found it to be boundless in healing children!

The rage is typically directed at the mother. Even if a child has been abused, assaulted or raped by the father or someone else, it is the mother whom the child blames because the mother did not keep him safe. The father will often not notice anything wrong with the child because it is the mother who is under attack. The child will often triangulate the parents by acting sweet and pitiful for "Daddy".

There are no accidents. The child breaking or banging into things are outward signs or signals of the child not "talking out" his anger. The child needs to connect feelings with actions and put them into words to release them in a safe/sane way.

 <u>After an outburst of rage,</u> let the child have time to settle and regain control with a minimum of five minutes of good sitting. Then direct the child over to sit on your lap for a processing and bonding session.
 To begin, the child sits on the parent's lap with one arm wrapped around the parent's back with a flat hand. The child's other hand is around the parent's waist with a flat hand. The child's head is in the bend of the parent's arm. The parent's hands are flat on the child's back. The parent makes strong loving eye contact with the child. The faces are six to eight inches apart. This is similar to a nursing position. It is a very nurturing and powerful position. (This is also the correct position for snuggle time.) A conversation takes place to process feelings with the parent guiding and encouraging with acceptance and understanding. Try to put yourself "in his shoes". The parent's eyes MUST remain filled with love or stop immediatly!

A sample conversation would be:
PARENT: <u>What happened</u>? (The wise parent sits quietly allowing the child time to think. The child needs to accept responsibility for whatever action occurred.)
CHILD : (The child needs to respond with "I was...") I was vacuuming and I banged the table with the vacuum.
PARENT: Yes you did, very good accepting responsibility. Give me five! <u>What were you feeling before you did that</u>?
CHILD: I was feeling mad I had to vacuum instead of play baseball. (The child must always respond in complete sentences.)
PARENT: I bet that did make you mad! Baseball is a lot more fun than vacuuming! <u>How did you handle that</u> mad <u>feeling</u>? (the parent validates the feeling, and then helps the child connect the action with the feeling.)
CHILD: I was feeling mad, so I took it out on the table by hitting it with the vacuum.
PARENT: <u>How did that work out for you</u>?
CHILD: Not very good! Now I have to fix the scrape on the table leg and I'm missing even more baseball because I got mad and blew it!
PARENT: <u>How do you think you might handle it better next time</u>?

CHILD : Next time I'll tell you how mad I am or go hit my pillow for a while first!
PARENT: That sounds like a good plan. I'll be proud of you when you get strong enough to talk out your feelings instead of act them out! (The parent validates the response with encouragement to handle future struggles better.

These few minute sessions occur throughout the day . They should always end with smiles and pizzazz. There is NO LECTURE! This is very important to keep communication open. A child needs to know he can come to you, tell you anything and everything, and you will guide him through the process and love him no matter what he did, said, or felt. All feelings are okay. It is what we do with those feelings that is not okay. Allow tears to flow unstopped, allow laughter to echo off walls. Allow and actually congratulate him for verbalizing his anger rather than acting it out. Telling you he wants to "kill the puppy" is far better than doing it!! Reward and encourage him to release feelings in words. This is vital.

Hold him through his fears, his tears, his rage and his joy. He will remember that you did. Some have said it was the best moments of their youth.
Writing what happened is done in a notebook for that purpose with the five underlined questions from page 88 written inside the cover to help him stay focused. One full page per incident is usually enough to help him think it through. After he writes it, I read, and then we discuss it. Remember, you have about two sentences before he tunes you out. Listen more than you talk.

Working it off with some physical activity, such as splitting wood (No you don't give a child an axe! We use wedges with a short handled sledge hammer), kneading bread, pounding nails, any activity that requires exertion, burns off that tension and helps the child discuss it calmly. Caution: do not give a violent child hammers, etc.

ALL WAS WELL; NOW WHAT HAPPENED?

When a child is waving red flags for help by noncompliance, disrespect, destructiveness, lack of eye contact, or no reciprocal smiles, it is time to come to his aid. Delving into the problem to help the child release the pain is very important. Feelings of anger often cover other emotions. It helps if you can discover what emotion is being covered. Sadness and/or fear are difficult emotions to bear and are often covered with rage. Feeling rage has customarily enabled the child to function. Deciding the cause of the acting out helps. Sometimes the child knows his problem. Sometimes, he honestly does not. Asking "Why?" is usually futile. Some of the common causes of acting out behaviors are:

Holidays are often tough times. Children often don't feel like they fit during these family times. Memories of past holidays return to haunt the child. Fantasies about how it could have been and expectations of how it "should be" all create an extremely difficult situation for the child to handle. This difficult time usually starts at Halloween and ends at the restart of school in January. This pattern usually continues yearly until the child gets stronger emotionally.

Anniversaries: date of adoption, any major move, injury, trauma. Painful memories can be stirred by a weather change such as snow if a traumatic event in the child's life happened during a snow storm. Halloween decorations in stores can disturb a child traumatized at Halloween. The smells of Christmas can start a turmoil inside a child moved at Christmas time. Documentation and observation may be needed in order to ascertain what is provoking the child.

Unconditional positive overload can happen in a grocery store or anywhere by a passer-by or relative commenting on how well-behaved your child seems. When a person says, "You are a good kid!", to a child whose self esteem is not healthy, the child will promptly let you know how wrong that comment was, usually by acting out to prove he is not a "good kid."

Secrets or "getting away" with something. When a child has a newly developed conscience, he often displays yucky behavior when his conscience is bothering him. Guilt is usually acted out until the child tells on himself, returns the stolen goods, or makes restitution for the misdeed.

Getting better too fast. Sometimes a child that has been doing well has to weird out when fear overtakes him. Seeing himself growing and changing, more quickly than his self esteem can handle, will cause a rapid downhill descent. The child may just need to feel miserable. This is an option certainly allowed. The child can feel miserable just as long as he likes. When he has stewed in his misery or self destructive behavior long enough, he may possibly pop out of it. Time in his room, with hourly loving contact by the parent, helps. Hugs and smiles, delivered to his door, let him know you still love him but also that your life is going on fine. Giving permission for a child to feel his feelings shows him that you respect those feelings. We sometimes feel sad, mad, scared, etc. We need to allow our children the same freedom to feel.

BELIEVE THAT THEY CAN MAKE IT!
KEEP THAT MESSAGE IN YOUR EYES!

CHAPTER TWELVE: BUILD SELF ESTEEM

The future belongs to those who believe in the beauty of their dreams.
                                            Eleanor Roosevelt

Self esteem, "whom we see ourselves to be," cannot be built until the bond is well on its way to being established. It is completely useless to tell an attachment disorder, ADD, ADHD or Tourette Syndrome child that he is great and you love them. Words do not change their distorted damaged image inside. He must see and feel it before the words mean anything.

Self esteem is the foundation on which a person's personality is built. There is a direct correlation between low self esteem and crime, violence, substance abuse, school drop outs and teen pregnancy. Building it is crucial to success! You are "the contractor" on this construction project of self esteem. What kind of contractor will you be? Will you be like Arnold Schwarzenegger or Pee Wee Herman?!

Self esteem is developed by internalizing the positive feelings projected by a loved one. Acceptance, not just in words but through the eyes, builds self esteem- rejection destroys it. I did not realize how much a child filters the world through his mother's eyes until one day my own eyes were opened. My seven year old daughter, Beth, was out watching the horse shoer. He looked up from his work into her amazing blue eyes and said "You sure do have pretty eyes." I remember the confused look on her face as she looked at me. Later I asked if she knew that she had very beautiful eyes. Her reply was a lesson for me I never forgot. She said, "People used to say that I had pretty eyes when I was with my other mom, I would look at her and her eyes would say that was not okay. Today when the shoer said I had pretty eyes I looked at you and your eyes said it was good. So is it okay if I have pretty eyes?" Your eyes speak volumes to your child. Be aware of what they say!

BRIBES, attempting to "buy the child's good behavior or happiness" does not create an environment that will allow a child to develop positive self esteem. You cannot build a positive relationship on bribes or threats.

DO NOT SAY -   "If you do that one more time, I'll ..." or
                  "I'll get you that if you will..." or
                  "If you will do ..., then I will...."

REWARDS AND BONUSES are little surprises given on occasion for above average accomplishments. They are given with love and pizzazz. In the beginning, rewards and bonuses should be for food, clothing, or necessities. As the child heals and develops better self esteem, higher levels of bonuses may be awarded.

OTHER SELF IMAGE BUILDING TOOLS include:
* Attractive photographs of the child on display and called attention to often
* Video of the child taken when the child is doing well. Edit the "Uglies"
* Calling the child by special nicknames such as Rocket Rose or Data.
* Displayed artwork and projects or photos of projects, even Lego® creations!
*Introductions including his name and special talent or current accomplishment

A child with low self esteem cannot handle a lot of new school clothes or a haul of toys at Christmas and birthdays. To show you that he cannot handle these things, he will quickly destroy them. Keep it simple and have him earn the privilege.

Catch the child doing something right! Behavior receiving the most pizzazz is the behavior he will repeat!

Avoid labeling (good or bad) "You are lazy"," You are clumsy," You are wonderful," "You are a terrific kid!" He knows he isn't "wonderful" or "terrific", and it makes you look phoney, like a liar or a fool. He will often blow out for days after one of these positive labels is bestowed on him! He believes he has to prove he isn't "wonderful" or whatever! He usually just agrees with the negative labels. Neither one works to build him up to believe in his abilities. DO NOT use them.

Use positive statements, with several conditions, after the child has shown some effort, to build the child's belief in his goodness, ability, and appearance. "What a nice smile you have today", "You are getting to be a good helper", "Right now you are doing a good job". " I see you are getting stronger".

A child who has not internalized a parent stronger than himself can not develop self esteem. Children with no conscience often have no self esteem.They will start to take you in when they start to trust you because you are strong.

Accept the Birth Parents They gave your child life. If they are "bad", so is your child. They are made from the same cloth! DO NOT trash the people who gave your child life, No Matter What! Yes, they made mistakes. Pray they get over them. Don't hurt your child with hate for these parents.

Create a Life Book In this picture album of the child's life, it should be from start to current. If there are no birth pictures, take a photograph of the hospital they were born in or put a star on a map by the country they were born in. The beginning of their life needs to have some kind of visual marker. Then each place they have lived, whether it be a hospital, insitution or a home, should have visual markers. Sometimes a child has been traumatized by being moved repeatedly and a timeline is necessary for the child to even visualize their past. The life book is to give them a sense of continuity for their life. It should not be split into two books, such as this is your life before you came to us, this is your life after you came to us. Visitng past families to gather information and pictures can be very helpful in learning to understand the child better. Some of the old photos past families may be reluctant to let go of, not wanting to lose their memories of the child. This is a sign of love that should be respected and honored. In that case, we take the parents out to lunch with the photos and color copy the photos so we each have a set.

Yesterday was Yesterday

It's important, as much as possible, to finish the day's business before bedtime and send the child to sleep on a peaceful note. Starting each new day with no hangovers from yesterday's deeds, helps the child to see each day as a new opportunity to improve rather than digging a hole deeper and deeper, day by day, until he is in a lose/lose situation. Sometimes, very creative techniques are the only way out for a child determined to dig a hole. For example, a child that has accumulated more pushups than is physically possible for that child to do may pay back hassle time owed by giving his dessert, toy, stereo, allowance, etc. to the person he has hassled. In this way he can pay promptly rather than accumulate a debt that's ongoing and building. A large debt can be broken into smaller amounts to be re-paid a certain amount each day.

Parents need to avoid bringing up past destruction, mistakes and bad decisions that the child has made. If your child brings up old, yucky memories, some good responses for the parents to use are: "Aren't you glad that's over!" or "I'm so glad you aren't that way any more!" "That was yesterday. We're working on today! How's today going to be?". This sort of response helps to bury the past.

It is essential for the parents to be healthy enough to forgive and forget each day's transgressions. Never let the sun set on anger. End each day with a loving hug. The message needs to be very clear that no matter what he has done, you still love him! It can be very damaging to the child's self esteem to have error after error brought to his attention repeatedly. An accumulation of dastardly deeds to be faced is depressing, degrading and can be overwhelming. Take one day at a time. Each "Good morning" is the start of a new day for you and your child.

REMEMBER: Your children are in good hands. They're in yours!

CHAPTER THIRTEEN: THE PROCESS- WHAT TO EXPECT

Life is either a daring adventure or nothing at all.
Helen Keller

The process of healing is not on a straight line from the bottom of the child's pathology to the top of success. It is more like a roller coaster, up and down, as he tries the new behaviors and returns to old comfortable (unacceptable) ones. He usually begins the ride in a great swooping desent as he fights your new controls and changes. Do not be discouraged as he rides the coaster to the bottom. Avoid the fear he will never return to the top which will dash your hopes time and time again. Stand back from the coaster, do not ride it with the disturbed child at the wheel. Maintain the tracks and safety equipment, so when he returns to the platform of sanity, you can embrace him with open arms rather than shaky legs and wild eyes. This is a difficult process for the child as well as the parent. Some wonder if it is worth the time and effort required. I have found it to be like potty training. It takes a lot of extra work in the beginning, lots of encouragement for each flush. Eventually we don't have to ask repeatedly, "Do you have to go?" Each interaction must be adjusted or encouraged in the beginning. The rewards are great. Is it worth the effort? Yes!

How do we know if it's working? - sign of success.

Start by doing what's necessary, then what's possible,
and suddenly you are doing the impossible .   St. Francis of
Assisi

The parents handle issues without being angry. When success starts to come through, you feel relief and peace and a decrease in the degree of anger you feel. The child is no longer in control. The parent is in control because the child can no longer "make" the parent angry . The parents are in control of their feelings.

Parents are taking care of themselves. That's really important, not only to get to success but to stay successful.

Child handles consequences with a good attitude. When you can say, "Because you broke this, you're going to owe me $20 . I have some chores you can do to pay it off." And the child says, "Oh, okay. I'd really like to get that paid off and get it off my back." When you have that kind of attitude coming through, it's great!

The child gets along better with siblings, and you notice peace and laughter in your home.

The child starts to do better in all environments - home and school. That doesn't mean grades. The relationship that the child has with the mom has a great impact on the relationship that he will have with their teacher now and a spouse later. If the child cannot learn to love his mother he will never learn to love his spouse. He will be lonely his entire life.

Good friendships. That doesn't mean that the friends he has chosen are the A students in the classroom. It means that he has friends that are continuing to be his friends and they have appropriate fun together.

The child sparkles. The dark circles around his eyes of stress are gone- replaced with a sparkle in the eyes and rosy cheeks. The smile on his face actually sparkles from his heart!

CONCLUSION

A child who has not allowed love into his heart for years, once he again embraces a loving relationship, has a tremendous capacity for love and giving. Helen Keller is an excellent example of an unattached child who learned to love humanity. I recommend reading her story and that of her healer, Ann Sullivan. Helen Keller said, "The most beautful things in the world cannot be seen or even touched... they must be felt with the heart".

IF A CHILD MUST BE MOVED, LETS DO IT RIGHT!
Transferring the Bond and Reintegrating Home From Care for Permanency Planning

When a seedling is transplanted, great care is taken to retain the soil around the roots to lessen the shock to the plant. The original nutrients it thrived on may be different than the new soil and the shock could be fatal. Just as the two soils must intermingle to buffer the shock for the seedling, so must two families' love intermingle inside a child's heart to aid in the difficult transition necessary as the bonding to the new family begins. How much more important is it that we transfer our children more carefully than our plants?!

A child in transition is a child in pain. Greg Keck, Ph.D., in his seminars on attachment and bonding often states, "The term 'moving' a child from one family to the next should be changed to 'traumatizing' so that the adults involved understand the pain they are causing." It is definitely not recommended to move a child, if the child is already at high risk for attachment disorder due to age (under the age of three), early trauma, abuse, ongoing pain or previous separation from birth mother, unless the child is in eminent danger. Re-traumatizing an already harmed child makes it much more difficult (in some cases impossible) for them to re-bond and develop a conscience.

In order for prospective parents to meet a child before deciding to commit, a group outing should be planned (church picnic, ballgame, etc.) The child should not be told they are being "examined" by a potential family or even told they are being traumatized by a move in the near future until it is iminently pending. The family can then see the child in the normal family environment without the child being in terror of possible rejection by a new family or the loss of the current one. The child is not told they are being evaluated by another family for fear of increasing anxiety around rejection issues, which damage self esteem. Giving a child weeks or months in "limbo", not knowing where they are going to go, fearful for their life, is emotional abuse. The prospective family should observe the child from a distance, as well as interact casually as any friendly person might at a picnic.

The most successful transition with the least trauma to the child is done by the new mother, and father if possible, living with the child in the place the child is currently living for a minimum of two weeks wether it be a foster home or institution. During this two weeks, the new mom focuses on establishing respect and creating and maintaining the heart to heart connection as outlined in Chapter Two and Three in part two of this book. The previous mom steps back from the nurturing role, maintaining the structure, providing meals, support, encouragment and instruction. This time invested inthe child's environment gives the new mother an understanding of some of the child's history, strengths, habits and weaknesses. In the future when the child discusses other children in that home, etc. the new mom will have a clear picture and be able to understand the child better in order to be more supportive and empathetic. This time together also gives the child time to connect in a familiar environment with the new mom. The new mother with the support of the present mom can focus completely on this vital transition time without the distractions of daily duties. Both moms laughing together, sharing time together and giving the child permission to love each sends a powerful message to the child that they are safe, that they have permission to love both moms, that the new mom loves them enough to want to understand them.

At the end of the transference period, the child then goes home with the new caregiver. This caregiver should make sure the child calls the previous caregiver every day for one week, then every other day for one week and gradually call less until the calls are only occasionally. Contact calls and cards should continue to be sent back and forth from child and caregiver on holidays and special occasions. To avoid confusion, we have the new mom take the title "Mom" and the previous mom becomes "Mom, Nancy or Mom, Pam, etc."

Expect either a "honeymoon period" of superficial charm for a period of minutes or weeks (up to 5 months) or be prepared for the grieving child to act out. They will usually act out their homesickness rather than talk about it for fear the new parents' feelings will be hurt or, because it activates old abandonment issues and causes more pain than the child wants to deal with. Often the child will say he doesn't want to talk to the previous family. Successful transition depends on the feeling of continuity. This "acting out," or depression, or denial is a signal for the new family to take control of the situation by modeling for the child and initiating contact with the previous caregiver promptly. The child receives a strong covert message that love is okay and that we confront feelings honestly. Telephone calls seem to be the easiest for the child to handle. Sometimes personal visits with past caregivers create more emotional turmoil than the child or the new caregivers can handle. Each child's needs are different so visits may be tried and continued, delayed or eliminated according to the child's needs.

Just as a carefully transferred seedling wilts and shows some regression, we expect the child to do the same. This regression can be lessened a great deal by giving the child permission to love. Some children repress all the good and loving progress from the previous environment and behaviorally and emotionally regress. This temporary regression is normal out of the pain of the move. The new parents often wonder if the previous parents taught the child anything at all! Parents must constantly remember that this child is acting out of pain, grief and fear. Tight structure, consequences given with empathy and powerful nurturing will ease the pain and help create a new bond with caregivers. Separation (school, day care etc.) from new caregivers must be delayed until child is well attached.

Successful transition is dependent on the ego strengths of the new parents to allow and actually encourage contact with the previous family. Feelings of jealousy or possessiveness can cut the "roots" and be fatal to the progress the child has made. This contact must be encouraged for an extended time until the child is really "locked in" to the new family. A child can handle feeling loved by more than one set of adults. Don't we expect them to love parents and grandparents? The more permission that is given to love, the more the child is able to love.

The most traumatizing method of moving a child is to have several visits with the new parents and then have a third party transport the child to the new home with no transference of the bond. Coldly severing the connection with no contact between homes creates the most pain and confusion for a child. During these visits, the new family usually treats the child as a guest. A good hostess is taught to make a guest feel comfortable by serving them. The focus is on making the guest happy. This is not a real life situation for the child. Later when they are brought into the home for the final trip, they are no longer a guest but a family member, expected to make their own bed, help with household chores, etc. They feel lied to, betrayed and ripped off. There was one child whose adopted family came from out of state to visit, staying in a hotel. The child was brought to them. The child visited by spending time in the pool, relaxing and lounging around. The child was very excited about the upcoming adoption. When the child was flown to their new home, he walked in and said, "Where's the big house you showed me before and where's the pool?" He was very angry. This was not what he had signed up for. This happens repeatedly by well meaning adoptive parents. We have found it much more successful for the parents-to-be to treat the child as a family member just as they will be for the rest of their life.

When a child feels a sense of loss or sadness at separating they often make a past parent or caregiver the "bad guy". The disturbed child may make false allegations of abuse or distort events in order to justify the pain of separation. They often blame separation pain and grief on a past caregiver. The new caregiver must be aware and cautious not to feed into this pathological method of handling sadness and loss by helping the child to be honest about their feelings.

A child in transition is a child in pain. Let's work together to lessen that pain and let the love grow. To love and re-bond is a gift of life!

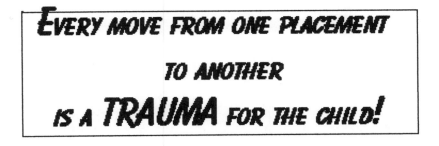

EVERY MOVE FROM ONE PLACEMENT TO ANOTHER IS A TRAUMA FOR THE CHILD!

APPENDIX A

TEMPLATE TO PREPARING AND SETTING UP YOUR HOME

SETTING UP YOUR HOME The home environment needs to be secured, i.e.,
made safe for your child and yourselves. Just as you would prepare by "child-
proofing" your home before bringing in a toddler or "puppy proofing" your home
before bringing in a pup, being proactive and avoiding more stress and hassles
puts you in control.

> You will need the following items:

> Shopping List for the Home
> > -Lock for a closet door
> > -Alarm for the child's bedroom door
> > -A pouch for your personal items
> > in the bathroom
> > -Music you find restful (without words,
> > preferably Mozart[1])
> > -A mini trampoline - try garage sales
> > -An entertaining book for you (like Chicken Soup for the Soul)
> Shopping List for the groceries. Your personal nutrition is important.
> > -Easy fruits; bananas, oranges, etc.
> > -Power Bars
> > -Cottage cheese, yogurt
> > -Chamomile tea, hot cocoa mix
> > -Apple sauce
> > -Tuna fish
> > -Vitamin B Complex

SEVEN DAYS TO HAVING YOUR HOME READY TO BEGIN

Day 1 Go to the stores and buy your supplies. Start taking the B Vitamins
and giving attention to what and how you are eating.

---

1 Mozart's music has been proven to have a soothing, healing effect on the nervous system and stimu
short and long term memory. It is excellent to set the tone in your home and to study to.

Day 2 With peaceful music playing, install the lock on the closet, the alarm on the bedroom door.

Day 3 (This can also be done on day 2) Put the family heirlooms in the locked closet along with the TV. Put your personal items from the bathroom in your pouch in your bedroom Explain to your child why the door alarm has been installed to his bedroom door.

It is important that you realize that tonight your child will test the door alarm. Your sleep will be disturbed, but you will now be aware of your child's activities at night. You will be empowered. You need to be prepared to carry through.

Day 4 Arrange uninterrupted time for yourself. Make a cup of tea, put on some Mozart music and take the test in Appendixes C,D,E for Post Traumatic Stress Disorder and Depression. Prepare for the safety of your pets.

Day 5 Stagger sleeping with your spouse, or get a sitter if you are a single parent, and get 10 to 12 hours of rest tonight.

Day 6 Set up your support system. Make a list of 10. Call them.

Day 7 Today take a walk, spend time with an entertaining book and get ready to take on the day. Tomorrow will be the first day of the rest of your life. You will be ready!

We all live busy lives. You have committed to implementing a new life style. The change will take a little time to become an established routine. It is my hope that you will be able to get started by using the Template right away. Now it is time to begin the work of powerful parenting. You will need to take care of yourself in order to effectively work with your child. It is important that you are getting rest, eating to nurture, and taking vitamins and minerals to heal. To be an effective, powerful parent you will need to support yourself. Your child will be testing the limits, trying to out-last you and wear you down in an effort to return to the old patterns that were not successful. It is your job to take care of yourself and, in turn then, have the resources to parent your child with love. Children learn what they see!

Attachment Disorder Symptoms

Child's name_____**Date**_____

Symptoms	Never	Some	Severe
Severe			
1. Superficially engaging & charming	___	___	___
2. Lack of eye contact on parents' terms	___	___	___
3. Indiscriminately affectionate with strangers	___	___	___
4. Not affectionate on parents' terms (not cuddly)	___	___	___
5. Destructive to self, others and material things (accident prone)	___	___	___
6. Cruelty to animals	___	___	___
7. Lying about the obvious (crazy lying)	___	___	___
8. Stealing	___	___	___
9. No impulse controls (frequently acts hyperactive)	___	___	___
10. Learning lags	___	___	___
11. Lack of cause and effect thinking	___	___	___
12. Lack of conscience	___	___	___
13. Abnormal eating patterns	___	___	___
14. Poor peer relationships	___	___	___
15. Preoccupation with fire	___	___	___
16. Preoccupation with blood & gore	___	___	___
17. Persistent nonsense questions & chatter	___	___	___
18. Inappropriately demanding & clingy	___	___	___
19. Abnormal speech patterns	___	___	___
20. Triangulation of adults	___	___	___
21. False allegations of abuse	___	___	___
22. Presumptive entitlement issues	___	___	___
23. Parents appear angry/hostile	___	___	___

Numbers 1-19 &23 (Cline,1979)

Depression Symptoms

Name_____   **Date**_____

Symptoms	Never	Some	
Severe			
1. Persistent feelings of sadness	____	____	____
2. Discouragement about the future	____	____	____
3. Limited ability to problem solve	____	____	____
4. Feelings of failure	____	____	____
5. Lack of satisfaction over things that used to satisfy	____	____	____
6. Feelings of guilt	____	____	____
7. Feeling like you are "being punished"	____	____	____
8. Disappointment in yourself or performance	____	____	____
9. Being critical of yourself for mistakes or weaknesses	____	____	____
10. Having thoughts or plans of suicide	____	____	____
11. Not feeling hopeful about the future	____	____	____
12. Inability to make decisions	____	____	____
13. Lack of concentration	____	____	____
14. Feelings of looking unattractive or old	____	____	____
15. Profuse tears or inability to cry	____	____	____
16. More easily annoyed or irritated	____	____	____
17. Loss of interest in other people	____	____	____
18. Difficulty getting started on projects	____	____	____
19. Inability to sleep restfully	____	____	____
20. Less energy/easily tired	____	____	____
21. Change in appetite, increase or decrease	____	____	____
22. Rapid weight loss or weight gain	____	____	____
23. Concern about physical problems, aches, pains	____	____	____
24. Loss of interest in sex	____	____	____

Post Traumatic Stress Disorder (PTSD)

Name_____   Date_____

Symptoms	Never	Some	Severe
Severe			
1. Exposure to event(s) involving trauma , threats or serious injury	___	___	___
2. Exposure to event(s) involving intense fear, helplessness or horror	___	___	___
3. Recurrent memories of traumatic event(s)	___	___	___
4. Recurrent distressing dreams of traumatic event(s)	___	___	___
5. Feelings of the trauma recurring	___	___	___
6. Intense distress at exposure to cues that symbolize part of the event	___	___	___
7. Physical response on exposure to cues symbolizing event	___	___	___
8. Efforts to avoid thoughts, feelings, or discussion of trauma	___	___	___
9. Efforts to avoid activities, places, or people that arouse memories	___	___	___
10. Inability to recall an important aspect of the trauma	___	___	___
11. Markedly diminished interest or participation in significant activities	___	___	___
12. Feelings of detachment or estrangement from others	___	___	___
13. Restricted range of facial expressions (affect)	___	___	___
14. Sense of hopelessness about the future	___	___	___
15. Difficulty falling or staying asleep	___	___	___
16. Irritability or outbursts of anger	___	___	___
17. Difficulty concentrating	___	___	___
18. Hypervigilance	___	___	___
19. Exaggerated startle response	___	___	___
20. Duration of the disturbance more than 1 month	___	___	___

PTSD Secondary Trauma

Name_____ **Date**_____

Symptoms	Never	Some	
Severe			
1. Realization that things between you and others have changed	___	___	___
2. You're no longer the same person as you were before	___	___	___
3. Inability to enjoy yourself with others in the same way	___	___	___
4. Feeling that you're unlike other people	___	___	___
5. Feeling disconnected from other people	___	___	___
6. Loneliness and alienation	___	___	___
7. Damaged sense of self worth/lowered self esteem	___	___	___
8. Feeling out of control emotionally	___	___	___
9. Development of physical problems	___	___	___
10. Excessive immersion in work	___	___	___
11. View of yourself and place in the world changes	___	___	___
12. Development of selective perception	___	___	___
13. More attuned to dangers	___	___	___
14. Loss of illusions of security	___	___	___
15. Loss of meaning in your existence	___	___	___
16. Loss of feeling of control	___	___	___
17. Development of victim identity	___	___	___
18. Fatigue and depression	___	___	___
19. Denial	___	___	___
20. Alternate between trying harder and giving up	___	___	___
21. Decrease in sex drive	___	___	___
22. Stress on significant relationships(marriage, etc)___	___	___	
23. Helplessness, hopelessness, and anger = rage	___	___	___

Appendix F   What makes me Lovable

This list, written by Paul, a 9 year old, is to clarify what respectful, responsible, and fun to be around means to a child.

RESPECTFUL
Doing things fast and snappy
Nice answers, "Yes, Mom!" and "Got it!"
Doing it Mom's way (Boss)
Good eye contact
Leaving other people's things alone
Letting other people finish their sentences

RESPONSIBLE (for body, own stuff, and chores)
Put your clothes away
Flush the toilet
Put tools away after chores
Take care of your body
Eating healthy foods
Taking care of your feelings in an OK way
Making your bed
Keep your room and closet clean
Finish work before play
Handle your school responsibilities

FUN TO BE AROUND
Smelling good
Clean shiny smile
Do chores promptly and right
Be polite
Eat nice
Nice manners
Quiet
Listen when people talk
Avoid arguments
Play calmly
Wear nice clothes
Offer to help others
Be honest and tell the truth

How do you Spell Relief?

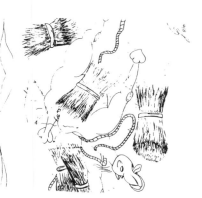

Medication information:
_____

My child should be responsible and ask for medication at the appropriate time, if not, please:

___Do Not remind (just note it)

___Do remind and assign an extra chore

Allergy and medical conditions child has
_____

My child _Does/Does not _ have a problem with bed wetting, urinating on carpets etc. **Emergency numbers** for doctors etc:
_____
_____

In case of emergency I hereby authorize anyone to administer first aid and any licensed physician to render necessary medical treatment to _____

age ____ signed _____

I will return to pick up my child at _____ time.

please do not share this information with my child. Knowledge is power and my child does not handle power well at this point. I appreciate your support and effort to help our family. THANKS!!!!

Res.pite- interval of rest or relief

Re.lief- the lifting of a burden or pain

This information presented by
Nancy Thomas   ncthomas@rof.net

What is Reactive Attachment Disorder?

RAD is a condition in which individuals have difficulty forming loving lasting relationships. They often have a nearly complete lack of ability to be genuinely affectionate with others. They typically fail to develop a conscience and do not learn to trust. They do not allow people to be in control of them due to this trust issue. They can be surface compliant for weeks if there is no loving relationship involved. With strangers they can be extremely charming and appear loving. Some adults misinterpret this as the child trusting or caring for them. If they cannot trust and love their own family that loves them, they will not trust and love a casual acquaintance! They do not think and feel like a normal person. Some famous people with RAD that did not get help in time: Saddam Hussein, Edgar Allen Poe, & Ted Bundy. One who did was Helen Keller.

Causes

Any of the following occurring to a child under 36 months of age puts a child at high risk for developing RAD:

- Abuse(physical, emotional, sexual)
- neglect
- sudden separation from primary caretaker (ie illness or death of mother or hospitalization of child)
- undiagnosed or painful illness such as colic or ear infections
- inconsistent or inadequate day care
- chronic maternal depression
- several moves or placements
- unprepared mothers with poor skills

Symptoms of Attachment disorde-

current & past   *Parents should mark issues*

- ☐☐ Superficially engaging & charming (phoniness)
- ☐☐ Lack of eye contact
- ☐☐ Indiscriminately affectionate with strangers
- ☐☐ lack of ability to give and receive affection (not cuddly)
- ☐☐ extreme control problems "sneaky"
- ☐☐ destructive to self and others
- ☐☐ cruelty to animals
- ☐☐ chronic crazy lying
- ☐☐ no impulse controls (stealing etc)
- ☐☐ learning lags and disorders
- ☐☐ lack of cause and effect thinking
- ☐☐ lack of conscience
- ☐☐ abnormal eating patterns
- ☐☐ poor peer relationships
- ☐☐ preoccupied with fire,blood & gore
- ☐☐ persistent nonsense questions and incessant chatter (jabbering)
- ☐☐ inappropriately demanding / clingy
- ☐☐ abnormal speech patterns(What?!)
- ☐☐ false allegations of abuse
- ☐☐ triangulation of adults (splitting)

Do Not leave this child alone with pets or kids

Tight structure and powerful nurturing from the real parents is the most effective way to get these high risk children back on track. You as the respite care provider have been chosen to be entrusted with the healing heart of this child. It is essential that this child not be given privileges that have not been earned at home. The basic privileges after a chore is completed may be:

- ◆ Playing alone with Legos or

- ◆ Reading- selected by an adult
- ◆ Drawing, coloring, watercolors
Extra privileges that this child has earned are:

_____

_____

_____

_____

Television, movies, nintendo, computor are NOT an option for this child! Sweets are a vital part of bonding and should only come from real parents, not earned, just given. This child is aware of this. Feel free to feed the rest of your family goodies so my child can see how other moms love their families. It will not harm my child. Do not deprive your family of their special things in front of my child. It makes RAD kids feel powerful and perpetuates the belief that adults are stupid suckers, easily manipulated. This keeps them from feeling safe which slows or halts the healing!

Goals of the child in care

- ◆ Make the relief parent happy with them
- ◆ Respectful (say "yes, mom..." or Mrs....)
- ◆ Responsible (jobs fast-snappy and right the first time not slow &sloppy)
- ◆ Fun to be around (smell good, eye contact, positive attitude, QUIET)

Goals of the relief parent

- ◆ Focus the child on the real parents (They are great! They love this kid! Tell the child, lots, how lucky they are!)
You are not their pal/buddy! You are the parents' pal/buddy!! They are the ones giving to this child who is draining them!!
- ◆ Support the real parents (remind them of their skills &caring. Let them know you understand . We all get tired!! Wise parents take care of themselves to avoid burnout and bad attitudes)
- ◆ Caution: game playing/triangulation These kids will lie to get one adult to feel sorry for them, to pit one adult against the other! Do not fall for this! Check it out! Do not pity them! They have parents and a loving home that they are trying to destroy. They are blessed!! Tell them!!
- ◆ Do NObonding activities with this child (loving eye contact, touch, smiles, sugar) Bonding, hugs, and snuggling must come from the real mom 'til the child is healed

Goals of the real parent

(definition of real parent-one who is there on a daily basis to cheer, support and guide a child through the obstacles of life NOT necessarily the birth parent)

- ◆ Relax
- ◆ Don't worry be happy
- ◆ Do not continually discuss the child
- ◆ Do something that's fun (you deserve it)
- ◆ Laugh lots (it is very healing)

BIBLIOGRAPHY

Bible, New International Version (1978) New York International Bible Society

Blankenhorne, David (1995) Fatherless America pg. 14, Harper Perrenial

Bowlby, J (1953) Child Care and the Growth of Love. Baltimore: Penguin Books.

Bowlby, J. (1973) Attachment and Loss: Vol. 2. Separation Anxiety and Anger. New York: Basic Books.

Bowlby, J. (1977a) "The making and breaking of affectional bonds: I. Aeitology and psychopathology in the light of attachment theory." British Journal of Psychiatry, 130, 201-210,

Cline, F.W., M.D. (1994) Hope for High Risk and Rage Filled Children: Reactive Attachment Disorder

Cline, F.W., M.D. (1982) Parent Education Text

Cline, F.W., M.D. (1979) Understand and Treating the Severely Disturbed Child

Cline, F.W., M.D. (1979) Understanding and Treating the Difficult Child

Magid, K. & McKelvey, C.A., (1988) High Risk: Children Without a Conscience, New York: Bantam Books.

Mansfield LG, & Waldmann,C.H. (1994)Don't Touch My Heart , Pinion Press

McKelvey, C.A. & STevens, JE. (1994) Adoption Crisis: The Truth Behind Adoption and Foster Care, Golden, Colorado: Fulcrum Press.

Verny, T. & Kelly, J. (1981) Secret Life of the Unborn Child. New York: Dell.
During my twenty five years of parenting and ten years of teaching and lecturing I have gleaned ideas and information from countless sources and incorporated them into my work, sometimes not knowing the original source. I hope there have been no serious omissions.

RECOMMENDED READING

Adopting the Hurt Child, by Gregory Keck, Ph.D. and Regina Kupecky,LSW. Pinon press1995

Give Them Roots ..Let Them Fly: Understanding Attachment Therapy, by Carole A McKelvey,MA the Attachment Center At Evergreen, INC   phone (303) 674-1910 web   www.attachmentcenter.org

Who's the Boss? Love, Authority, and Parenting by Gerald Nelson,&Richard Lewak

High Risk: Children Without a Conscience, by Dr. Ken Magid and Carole McKelvey Bantam Books 1989

Understanding and Treating the Severely Disturbed Child 1979
    also
Parent Education Text "What shall we do with this child" 1982
    also
Hope for High Risk and Rage Filled Children 1991
    also
Conscienceless Acts Societal Mayhem 1995
above four books by Foster Cline M.D.
PO Box 2380, Evergreen CO 80439

Holding Time, by Martha Welsh M.D. Simon and Schuster 1988

The Miracle Worker, by William Gibson Bantam Books/Perma 1962

The Secret Life of The Unborn Child, by Thomas Verny M.D.
Dell publishing a division of Bantam 1981

Parenting Teens with Love and Logic, by Foster Cline, M.D. and Jim Fay,
 Pinon Press1992

Parenting with Love and Logic,by Foster Cline,M.D. and Jim Fay, Pinon Press1990

Primal Wound, by Nancy Verrier, Gateway Press, 1994

Therapeutic Parenting it's an Attitude,
by Deborah Hage web   http://www.debrahage.com/pwp Phone - 970-468-0339

Touching (the Human Significance of the skin), by Ashley Montagu
Harper and Row publishers

Seminars Available by *Nancy Thomas*

Rebuilding the Broken Bond

This fun and informative two day workshop will define attachment disorder and share in depth survival skills for succeeding with the unattached child. When *love* is not enough there **are** solutions! These techniques can make: kids more fun to be around, your life easier, and their lives more successful!

How Do We Spell Relief ?

R-e-s-p-i-t-e C-a-r-e: lifting of a burden or pain. All the "how tos" of setting up and performing kids' therapeutic respite care to support parents and get help before it is too late!

Self-Esteem: Transplant Surgery & Post-Op Care

An exciting workshop filled with practical, effective blueprints to rebuild the broken foundation of a child's self esteem. Powerful tools developed, and proven on severely emotionally disturbed children will be presented.

Coming Home: The Art of Reintegration

Enjoy learning how to re-connect the puzzle pieces of the separated family. Discover skills to jump start all of you for success! A great training for new adopters as well as those re-joining a family.

Bonding Right From The Start

This 1 1/2 hour class on parenting infants and the importance of bonding, shares how to prevent raising a child without a conscience. Includes interventions for high risk babies. Your baby can be a winner!

Captive in the Classroom

This class is for teachers, parents and school administrators. Powerful techniques will be shared for redirecting damaged, discouraged and undisciplined students. The clear concise tools needed to turn them toward success will be presented. Information on how to identify high risk kids will be given as well as classroom interventions that WORK!

Families by Design, PO Box 2812, Glenwood Springs, CO 81602
Phone 970 984-2222   e-mail ncthomas@rof.net

THE LATEST TOOLS FOR PARENTS AND PROFESSIONALS SEEKING ANSWERS FOR ATTACHMENT PROBLEMS IN CHILDREN

When Love Is Not Enough - $12, 114 page guide to parenting children with Reactive Attachment Disorder (RAD) and other emotional disturbances. This book, by Nancy L. Thomas, has a clear focused plan for parenting disturbed children back to health. It is filled with specialized parenting tools for parents looking for answers. If you want to make a difference in the life of a child, this method will do it. Part one of the book includes understanding RAD, its causes and high risk warning signs. Part two has the solutions, including   one dozen dynamic parenting techniques put together in a workable plan with lots of how to's.

Some things parents are saying -
"Your book has been the first hopeful reading that I have come across. I loved the practical suggestions. Thank you for writing such an encouraging book for us parents out in the 'cold'". Anne M., Renton, WA
"The parenting techniques are working and at the very least I am in charge of my home again. And I have hope......Thanks." Tracy P., Corvallis, MT

Rebuilding the Broken Bond - $30, This two video set has four hours of hope and humor as a fully developed parenting plan for emotionality disturbed children is shared. It is presented by internationally known speaker and author, Nancy Thomas. This set is filled with tools and techniques that are powerfully effective in rebuilding the bond and regaining control of children with RAD, ADD, ADHD, bipolar disorder and Tourette's Syndrome, as well as other behavior problems. The high points from a 13 hour presentation were gleaned to provide in-home training from the comfort of your own chair to help parents and professionals understand and help heal the heart of a wounded child.

Circle of Support - $15, This is a 1 hour newly updated video to be shown to family and friends who do not live with the emotionally disturbed child. These outsiders often see a very different child from the one the parents face on a daily basis! This often creates hard feelings and misunderstandings between adults. RAD is clearly explained. Encouragement and ideas to support the parents are powerfully presented. Parents have found this video very helpful to access much needed support.

Healing Trust: Rebuilding the Broken Bond - $18.95, These
two audio cassettes have three hours of listening that can be enjoyed at home or as you drive (for busy parents). Laugh along with Nancy Thomas as she explains Reactive Attachment Disorder (RAD) and the twelve powerful parenting techniques she has used successfully for many years to guide disturbed children toward emotional health and happiness. Many parents have shared with us that they enjoy listening to these tapes over and over to renew hope, gain more encouragement and fine tune the specialized parenting skills to help their child.

Captive in the Classroom - $40, This three hour video set,
professionally produced, presents powerful techniques for redirecting difficult, defiant and disruptive students. Clear concise tools to identify emotionally disturbed children and youth who
have the potential for violence are included.
Effective classroom interventions for
emotionally disturbed students are clearly
explained.
Educators can regain respect and the honor
that they deserve as the head of the class.
Many parents have purchased this tape to
share with their children's teachers to save
their sanity while making them a vital part of
the healing team.

Give Me a Break- $29.95, We are so excited
about this addition of tools to help with these difficult children! This professionally produced 2 1/2 hour video set provides information caregivers need in order to be highly effective in providing therapeutic respite/relief. Understanding and skills to perform this vital work are presented in a light hearted way to lift heavy hearts! Learn where to find these special people and how to train them to do this vital part of the teamwork!

Check out our web site at:
www.attachment.org

Biology of Behavior - $18.95, This two and a half hour audio tape set explores the physical causes of behavior and attention problems in children. It is filled with fascinating facts and identifying factors to spot a child who can benefit from this super nutrient program developed by Dianne Craft, MA, CNHP. As a special education teacher for over 25 years, she researched the backgrounds of out-of-control students and found interesting physical similarities. Then she searched and discovered the nutritional answers to the puzzle she had found. This is not a diet! It is well researched nutritional additions to include with what your child is eating now. She has used this super nutrient program with over 700 students and found improvement in 100%.

Handbook of Attachment Interventions - $49.95, 277 page book, published by Academic Press, shares information on clinical interventions for attachment disorders. The book meets this need by providing information on diverse patient populations across different therapeutic philosophies, while providing specific techniques for treating attachment disordered children and their familles. This handbook includes contributions by Terry Levy and Mike Orlans, authors of the well known book, Attachment, Healing and Trauma, John Alston, MD, the leading psychiatrist in differential diagnosis between bipolar disorder and RAD, Paula Pickle, the director of The Attachment Center at Evergreen, Nancy Thomas, internationally known Therapeutic Parenting Specialist and eight other outstanding leaders in this field.

99 Ways to Drive Your Child Sane - $10, 102 pages guaranteed to bring a smile to your face and laughter back into your home. Children with attachment problems drain the laughter out of a family. This little book is generously filled with gems of outrageous interventions guaranteed to keep you laughing while you are learning how to keep the fun in parenting. Author, Brita St. Clair, ingeniously draws on her 14 years as a special education teacher and 19 years as a therapeutic treatment parent dealing with severely emotionally disturbed children.

❄ ❄

COMING-MARCH 2002! Dandelion On My Pillow, Butcher Knife Beneath, the story of triumph and tragedy of life with children who suffer from emotional disturbances. The stories of kids who killed and learned to love and care again will warm your heart! Thrill to the stories of this family with the courage and unending love to save them from a life of crime and loneliness. Written by Nancy, Terena and Beth Thomas.

Order Form

Name_____

Shipping

Address_____City_____State_____

ZIP _____ Phone _____

_____ copies of the book When Love is Not Enough at $12 each   _____
A guide to parenting children with Reactive Attachment Disorder

_____copies of the video set Rebuilding the Broken Bond at $30 each   _____
This set, four hours, presents a fully developed parenting
plan for emotionally disturbed children. Presented in a humorous
format with tools and techniques fully explained in a workable plan.

_____copies of book Dandelion On My Pillow, Butcher Knife Beneath $19.95   _____
The story of triumph and tragedy of life with children with RAD

_____ copies of the newly updated video Circle of Support at $15 each   _____
60 minute video explains RAD & gives great support ideas for
friends and family. Designed to be supportive to the family.

_____ copies of Healing Trust: Rebuilding the Broken Bond audio $18.95 ea   _____
Two humorous cassettes, three hours, explains RAD & 12 powerful
parenting skills to guide a disturbed child toward emotional health.

_____ copies of the video Captive in the Classroom   at $40 each   _____
This set, 3 1/2 hours, presents powerful techniques for redirecting
difficult students. Clear concise tools to identify disturbed children &
save teachers' sanity are included.

_____ copies of the Give Me A Break video at $29.95 each   _____
This video set, 2 1/2 hours, provides information babysitters need to be
highly effective to provide therapeutic respite/relief. Understanding and
skills to perform this vital work are presented.

_____ copies of the Biology of Behavior audio at $18.95 each   _____
This audio explores the physical causes of behavior and attention
problems in children and provides an effective treatment ideas.

_____ copies of Handbook of Attachment Interventions $49.95 each   _____
12 authors (including Nancy Thomas) share their experience and insight
on clinical interventions for attachment disorder with specific techniques.

_____ copies of 99 Ways to Drive Your Child Sane booklet at $10 each   _____
by therapeutic mom, Brita St Clair. Wild ideas to add hysterical humor to
a home with a disturbed child, includes lots of great "one liners"!!

Please include shipping/handling charges as follows: sub total   _____

Order totals	Add
Up to $30	$ 4
$31 - $45	$ 6
$46 - $90	$ 9
$91 - $150	$12

S & H   _____

Total enclosed   _____

Payable to: Families by Design
PO Box 2812
Glenwood Springs, CO 81602

Write for volume discounts

We accept Discover, Visa & MasterCard - to order please call 970-984-2222